Political Kinship in Pakistan

Anthropology of Kinship and the Family

Series Editors: Murray Leaf (University of Texas at Dallas) and Dwight Read (University of California, Los Angeles)

Mission Statement

Kinship relations create the foundation of human systems of social organization. In order to understand kinship as a system of social relations, it is necessary to examine the structural organization of terms. The *Anthropology of Kinship and the Family* series is based on the notion that the underlying ideas of kinship can have more immediate importance than the linguistic symbols, as these ideas are evident in all behaviours involved in kin relationships. This series encourages contributors to highlight the social and conceptual power of kinship terminologies. Scholarly monographs and edited collections that focus on old topics associated with kinship, such as family organization and rules of marriage, and new approaches to the study of kinship systems are welcome.

Books in Series

Political Kinship in Pakistan: Descent, Marriage, and Government Stability by Stephen M. Lyon

Ethnic and National Identity in Bosnia-Herzegovina: Kinship and Solidarity in a Polyethnic Society by Keith Doubt and Adnan Tufekčić

Political Kinship in Pakistan

Descent, Marriage, and Government Stability

Stephen M. Lyon

LEXINGTON BOOKS
Lanham • Boulder • New York • London

Published by Lexington Books
An imprint of The Rowman & Littlefield Publishing Group, Inc.
4501 Forbes Boulevard, Suite 200, Lanham, Maryland 20706
www.rowman.com

6 Tinworth Street, London SE11 5AL, United Kingdom

Copyright © 2019 by The Rowman & Littlefield Publishing Group, Inc.

All rights reserved. No part of this book may be reproduced in any form or by any electronic or mechanical means, including information storage and retrieval systems, without written permission from the publisher, except by a reviewer who may quote passages in a review.

British Library Cataloguing in Publication Information Available

Library of Congress Cataloging-in-Publication Data Available

ISBN 978-1-4985-8217-9 (cloth)
ISBN 978-1-4985-8219-3 (pbk)
ISBN 978-1-4985-8218-6 (electronic)

*Dedicated to the memory of Yoshiaki Fukushima 義昭 (1950–2014)
A man who knew the importance of family and marriage.*

Contents

List of Figures	ix
Acknowledgments	xi
1 Kinship and Politics	1
2 Strong Man Politics, Pakistan and Methods	23
3 Waves of Elites	33
4 Descent, Marriage, and Building Networks	47
5 Kinship and Conflict Management at the Local Level	63
6 Landed Elite	81
7 Industrialist and Populist Challengers	97
Conclusion: Systemic Resilience and Robustness	113
References	123
Index	133
About the Author	137

List of Figures

Figure 6.1	Network Map of Elected Officials from the 2013 Elections	85
Figure 6.2	Elected Officials from the 2013 Elections with Lineages Collapsed	86
Figure 6.3	The Kinship Network of the Chaudhrys of Gujerat, Including the Influential Attock Family Led by Major Tahir Sadiq	91
Figure 6.4	The Kinship Network of the Chaudhrys of Gujerat (Including the Cluster Based in Attock)	92
Figure 6.5	The Bhutto Kinship Network	93
Figure 7.1	The Sharif Kinship Network	99
Figure 7.2	The Kinship Network of the Sharifs	100
Figure 7.3	Imran Khan Kinship Network	103
Figure 7.4	Imran Khan Kinship Network Showing Clusters of Related Families	104

Acknowledgments

This book would not have been possible without the sustained and enthusiastic support and hospitality of many friends in Pakistan. I would, therefore, like to express my profound gratitude for the care and affection that numerous people in Pakistan have shown me for almost four decades. I have enjoyed the friendship and wisdom of so many people; it's impossible to name them all, but I would be remiss if I did not explicitly thank some of my Bhaloti family in Attock District, Punjab: Malik Asif Nawaz, Malik Bilal Mehdi, Malik Imran Khan, Malik Amir Afzal, Malika Faroukh Sultan, Malika Tahira, Malik Wajjid Hussain, Malik Awais Ali, and Malik Wasif Nawaz. I have been fortunate to be adopted into a Lahori family as well, and will forever owe a debt to Malik Tayyab Yazdani, Rubina Yazdani, Danish Yazdani, Hamza Yazdani, Rameesha Yazdani, and Alisha Yazdani. Beyond those people who have adopted me into their families, I have been privileged with the acceptance and support of countless rural and urban Punjabis over the years who have kept me fed, clothed, entertained, and alive.

The research for this book would not have been possible without the financial and logistical support of the Durham Global Security Institute, the Department of Anthropology at Durham University, the International Water Management Institute, and the Institute for the Study of Muslim Civilisations at the Aga Khan University in London. Over the years, I have presented draft versions of almost every chapter of this book at seminars, workshops, and conferences in which my colleagues have provided invaluable feedback. I am particularly grateful for the participants of successive Pakistan Workshops in the Lake District, England, and the regular meetings of the Society for Anthropological Sciences. I would like thank especially Muhammad Aurang Zeb Mughal, Elisabeth Kirtsoglou, Hamza Hasan, Robert Layton, Murray Leaf, Dwight Read, Douglas Hume, Pnina Werbner, Sana Haroon, Martin Sökefeld, Iain Edgar, Mohammad Waseem, David Henig, Masako Kudo,

Ayaz Qureshi, Mwenza Blell, Marta Bolognani, Bruce White, Ali Khan, Michael Fischer, Alan Bicker, Alan Nicol, Arif Anwar, Leif Stenberg, Jonas Otterbeck, Nadir Cheema and the late Mariam Abou Zahab.

Lastly, I am fortunate to have the support of my non-Pakistani family. I was lucky to have grown up in households that valued curiosity and knowledge. My parents and siblings, in their different ways, have encouraged and inspired me to continue to learn and develop throughout my life. My children, Tadashi and Tomiyo, have had to put up with my frequent extended absences while I disappear off to a country they only know through unhelpful media and possibly romanticized accounts from me. My partner, Chisaki Fukushima, has been a wonderful interlocutor who has had a significant impact on the direction of all of my research for almost two decades. Needless to say, I am solely responsible for the faults and weaknesses in this book.

Chapter 1

Kinship and Politics

The distribution of power has been a persistent interest in philosophy and social sciences from the very beginning. Whether from a "how-to" perspective about amassing or holding power justly (or not), or an analytical view from afar intended to make sense of *how* power is distributed, held, gained, lost, and used, people have long tried to figure out more reliable ways of predicting and explaining phenomena of power. Understanding the mechanisms, meanings and consequences of power in human societies remains one of the abiding interests across all social sciences, nowhere more so than when the societies in question are armed with nuclear weapons and state regimes that look alarmingly unstable both from afar and up close. My goal here is not to provide an analytical theory that can be used to *explain* all, or even most, societies, but rather to demonstrate the way one part of the world both *establishes* and *resists* control over groups of people. Pakistan is a relatively young state whose people share overlapping, ancient histories. It's a country that is infamous for its political instability and corruption, yet it steadfastly refuses to slip into the realm of "failed" state, like its neighbor Afghanistan or some unfortunate countries in other parts of the world. For all its flaws, the Pakistan state persistently demonstrates an impressive level of continuity and stability *despite* the sometimes abrupt and disruptive changes in leadership. Pakistan provides an invaluable example of the ways in which cultural systems, specifically those that operate in and around kinship relations, provide powerful idioms for social organization that can and do contain the power of the state in ways that can be both subtle and crude, perhaps simultaneously.

One of the many take-home lessons from a detailed analysis of Pakistani politics is that the boundaries of public and private, national and local, individual and collective are all contestable and deniable. Throughout this book, I use insights gained from extended study of a small, relatively insignificant village in northern Punjab, to make sense of actions and events that affect the entire country. Using the same techniques to understand local land disputes and the formation of coalitions in governments may seem an intellectual stretch too far for some people, but the fact is that making sense of national electoral politics in Pakistan necessarily means unpicking the complex network of relationships that bind ostensibly locally focused political networks together. Unlike some other well-established electoral democracies in which shared ideologies can provide the foundation for the imagined electoral communities required to win the highest offices, in Pakistan, the evidence would suggest that political party ideologies are neither coherent nor compelling enough to serve that role. Instead, the binding ideology is one of kinship. Mutual, reciprocal obligation that comes from being *kin* may be the only glue that holds some movements together in Pakistan. The truly remarkable feature of using kinship as the binding mechanism to link otherwise unconnected political networks,[1] is that it makes no assumptions about mutual affection or agreement. Kin can and do fight with one another, while still satisfying kin obligations. Land disputes between close kin are common, possibly even *quasi-obligatory* in rural Pakistan, yet that doesn't negate kinship obligations in other domains of interaction. Such relations can be strained to breaking point between two individuals, but the relations are *not* dependent on *dyadic* pairs between any two people. They are fundamentally characterized by systemic relations between groups of people. I may despise one of my mother's brother's sons, (which, for the record, I do not), but that doesn't mean I will sever relations with my mother or that she will sever relations with her brother. In other words, kinship provides a resilient system of relations that can deal with high levels of conflict and disruption in formal leadership role-holders. Not only does this help us to better understand Pakistani state politics, but it also moves us closer toward a coherent understanding of the interplay between social and cultural systems in bureaucratic and state contexts.

POWER AND APPROACHES

Anthropologists, as well as other social scientists, were keen to understand how resources could be distributed and conflicts managed in the absence of formal regulatory institutions or roles. Perhaps the one thing that most undergraduate anthropology students retain about nineteenth-century armchair anthropologists is that they very quickly realized that with or without states, police, or armies, it was possible to wage war, resolve disputes, and regulate behaviors in all societies. Developing cross culturally robust theories to account for such regulation has been an ongoing process and, like other areas within the discipline, there is disagreement. Radcliffe-Brown (1957) and

Evans-Pritchard (1940, 1937) provided influential models for making sense of so called acephalous societies that lacked states.[2] This work was significant for a variety of reasons. That generation of scholars sought to build a working theory of society based on empirical observation of the functional consequences of social institutions and their interactions. Despite a good deal of criticism leveled at the structural functionalist school of British social anthropology, a great many social anthropologists in the twenty-first century continue to be noticeably influenced by some of the *a priori* assumptions about what constitutes the field, which methods to adopt, the appropriate harmony of observer and participant. Many of the resulting ethnographic accounts have dropped of the scientific aspirations of the structural functionalists, but they continue, by and large, to aspire to be able to make reliable inferences and generalize about the *whole* communities or societies upon which they are based. Ethnographers continue to feel the need to spend extended periods of time in the field, because there remains an almost zealous devotion to the empirical roots of our discipline.

There are social scientists who have focused on power to the extent that they see everything through that prism. Foucault (1977, 2008, 1978) has become something of a godfather to many political anthropologists who focus on discourses of power and knowledge that construct and regulate bodies and create docile citizens, or conversely challenge the constraining regulations of biopolitics, however pointless the revolution may be (given that regardless of which group winds up on top, the individual is *always* constrained and controlled by the discourses of power).

I too have examined power throughout my academic career. I have tried to understand how conflicts and resources are managed and part of that examination has been carried out by paying attention to the points in which individuals and groups clash. Knowing what people are prepared to fight about is a useful entry point into trying to better understand what matters most to them and what they consider right, wrong, thinkable, and unthinkable. In earlier work I discussed the interconnected patron-client relationships that are ubiquitous across Pakistan (Lyon 2004) and conflict mediation processes through customary social institutions (Lyon 2002, 2004). However clumsily my efforts, I was attempting to develop a coherent representation of communities in which asymmetrical relationships of power provided a foundational model of society. As my work has progressed more recently, I have broadened my attention to the cultural systems that make such foundational models possible. Kinship has always figured prominently in my analyses because all of my sustained work in Pakistan has been carried out with individuals who repeatedly refer to their kin groups. Evans-Pritchard isn't the only anthropologist to say that we should follow the preoccupations of the people with whom we work, but his account of his shift from Nuer politics to Azande witchcraft (Evans-Pritchard

1976) was the first compelling argument that I read that persuaded me that as an anthropologist, my own preoccupations had to be subordinate to those of my "people."[3] Despite being utterly persuaded, however, I noticed that E-P was actually *still* fundamentally following the ways that people managed conflict. For the Nuer, the conflicts revolved around cattle and the acephalous nature of their social organization meant conflicts were managed in very *ad hoc* ways that required a careful analysis of agnatic lineages. The Azande, with a more formally organized system of leadership, instead relied on systems of divination and witchcraft to both attack others and discern who was attacking them. In both cases, he was interested in power.

To be sure, there are real limitations to an unsophisticated application of structural functionalism. Following World War II, anthropologists realized that a tidy structural functionalist model couldn't account for their ethnographic observational data. Individuals exerted their own interests onto their decision making and made use of more than one set of values and principles to assess their contexts. Bott's (1957) classic study of domestic relations demonstrated that the distribution of responsibilities was directly affected by the people with whom they were connected more than the fact that they were connected to each other. So the effect of being part of a complex network triggers different responses to the same cultural values and expectations. These effects aren't adequately incorporated within an approach that exaggerates the focus on the relationship between social institutions. Others at the same time were clearly searching for better ways to integrate individual decision making and strategizing (see especially Barnes 1969; Turner 1958; Gluckman 1955).

In the areas in which I've worked in Pakistan, my interests have never veered far from power, despite meandering around kinship (e.g. Lyon 2005, 2010; Lyon, Jamieson, and Fischer 2015; Lyon and Mughal 2016) or conceptual models of nature (Lyon and Mughal 2017, 2019) or other areas. This is because issues of competition and cooperation are ever present in the field and while some ethnographic sites emphasize peaceful negotiation, Pakistani communities exhibit a high tolerance for the theatricality of conflict. Shouting and threatening gestures, if not every day occurrences, are frequent and mostly unremarkable. I once went with some friends from a little village to a fast-food restaurant in Islamabad. We had some of the younger children with us, no more than 8 years old. I was watching one of the little boys play with the other children in a play area. There was another little boy who was pushing his fist into my "nephew's" cheek. My nephew was looking glum but not reacting. I told the other boy, as gently as I could, not to do this aggressive thing he was doing. Both boys stared at me in confusion. One of my "brothers" came to see what was causing distress and when he saw, he laughed. He told me not to worry about it. I asked what our nephew should do and he replied that it didn't matter, maybe hit the other boy, maybe not. It was children playing. I asked what his sister, the boy's mother, would say if she were present. He laughed again and said that if our nephew's mother were present, she would tell her son to hit the other boy very hard in the face. I laughed and said I was sure that our sister wouldn't be so harsh and everyone else laughed and said that was Punjabi childhood—mothers egging their children on to fight more aggressively than the other kids in the play-ground. My point isn't that Punjabis are *more* violent than people in other societies, but rather they may be more accustomed to the performance of violence. It is more visible and present in their lives than in some other places. Hence, my interest in conflict and violence.

As I have explored issues related to conflict and violence, one theme has persistently figured prominently: kinship. Through all of the instances of violence and conflict, I return again and again to the people mobilizing their kin or mobilizing *against* their kin to compete over material and symbolic resources. The "prizes" in these competitions are often expressed in ways that interweave kinship, family, and household into the outcomes. People do things for the honor and protection of their lineage, household, ladies, ancestors, or children. These may all be proximate causes of conflict, but they are real motivators of violence and action.

This book brings together aspects of kinship that bear on conflict and vice versa. It is about contestation of power, but through prism of kinship. People don't capitalize on their networks by invoking common aspirations for power, but they can and do mobilize those networks by invoking ideas of mutual obligation and responsibility that are triggered by kinship connections. Consequently, this is an examination of the *consequences* of kinship through its myriad instantiations in the everyday lives of ordinary and extraordinary people.

RIVAL FOUNDATIONS OF POWER

Early on, anthropologists of South Asia were keen to try and understand some of the more obvious forms of hierarchical ranking and situate these within broader political relationships with the state. The concept of *varna,* or caste, in Hinduism, provided a rich source of data to unpick the complex social relations between groups. The fact that there appeared to be some legacy vestiges of *varna* in formerly Hindu converts to Islam, Christianity, Sikhism, and Buddhism, meant that explanations for *varna* might at least be partially relevant for most populations in India. This key Indian social institution has been analyzed from functional and materialist economic-oriented studies that prioritize the economic aspects of the occupational specialisms that are integral to *varna* systems, seen in the work of Bouglé (1971) and Leach (1962). Arguably the approach that has captured more attention since the 1960s has been driven by a focus on ritual and dogma, epitomized particularly in the seminal work of Dumont (1970). Materialist and symbolic entry points to *varna* agree on one thing, however, at its heart, it is a hierarchical system that regulates differential control over resources. Even in the era when structural functionalist British social anthropology dominated the study of areas that were then part of the British Empire, however, there were those who refused to subscribe to either a purely materialist or purely symbolic take on the hierarchies of India. Hocart (1950), in work that was well ahead of its time, offered a productive way of understanding *varna* systemically in relation to other institutions of power, notably kingship and kinship. These important social institutions, he argued, worked at cross purposes and effectively prevented any single one of them from consolidating power. Each institution operated as a "natural" check on the power of the others. At its essence, Hocart's attempt to understand how power is accumulated while simultaneously being prevented from all consuming accumulation, is what this book is about.

In contemporary Pakistan, there are obvious institutions that should control the country. The civil service is extremely large and provides high-quality, secure employment to some of the best educated people in the country. The military is one of the largest in the world, in terms of people, and has intermittently run the country directly for several decades of Pakistan's short history. The elected political leaders are typically powerful individuals with ostensibly huge bases of support. The country has singularly fallen short of establishing stable governments, of any sort. It has hobbled along through some relatively successful political regimes and, as of 2013, seems finally to have cracked the curse that seemed to be preventing a smooth transition of power between elected governments. It has had some military rulers who managed to stay in positions of authority for around a decade, but none of them have really managed to establish a firm hold over the political reins of the state. Pakistan has somehow managed to prevent both autocratic and democratic entrenchment of power.

Throughout this book I set out to answer the paradox of Pakistan's seeming dual nature. It is a deeply hierarchical place that prevents groups at the top of the hierarchies from consolidating unchallenged power. The key to this lay in the rival power bases represented by kinship and the state. I don't address caste as a separate institution, as Hocart might, because in a Muslim context, while *varna* is vestigially interesting, it manifests itself through kinship rather than through a distinct ritualistic system. I go one step further, however, in unpacking the competing concepts *within* kinship that mitigate against overly consolidated kin groups. In other words, just as *kinship* must be understood as a power institution that challenges and checks the *state,* the twin tools for reproducing kinship, *descent* and *alliance*, both complement and check one another. The result is that neither descent groups nor marital alliance groups hold complete sway over kin groups. Instead, they provide a dynamic landscape in which individuals and groups can and do maneuver to minimize negative and maximize positive outcomes.

The puzzles surrounding Pakistani hierarchies and power relationships have held my attention for several decades and while this book is an argument for *how* and *why* things are the way they are in Pakistan, there will always be more details to unravel and pick over to try and genuinely understand this enigma of a country.

PAKISTAN'S FRAGILITY

The seemingly precarious nature of Pakistan's continued existence has inspired a peculiar genre of social and political science literature. The title of Tariq Ali's (1983) famed book stated the problem succinctly, *Can Pakistan Survive?: The Death of a State.* Not only was Pakistan doomed to succumb to the forces of revolution, Ali argued, but it was never a necessary to state to begin with. The challenge to national cohesion is not simply one of *peripheral* disengagement, but includes a perception that even the *core* struggles to cohere around the central idea of Pakistan (see Lustick 2011 for an interesting twist on the usual simulation scenarios of disgruntled peripheries breaking away from dominant core provinces). Rather unusually, Pakistan was the culmination of a collection of ideas around religious nationalism that owed little to contiguous geography, shared language or other cultural traditions.

Alavi's (1972, 1983) seminal work on the composition of Pakistan's power elite identified three groups of control: the large farmers, the indigenous bourgeoisie, and the metropolitan bourgeoisie (Alavi 1972). Alavi's model of competing interest groups is not without its problems (see McCartney 2019; Akhtar 2019; Zaidi 2014), the principle of competing interest groups that both prevent absolute control by any single party while simultaneously obstructing the development of stable civil society organizations elsewhere in the country, appears sound. Much as Hocart identified rival social institutions that challenged the total control of historical India, Alavi's insightful contribution on the ways that the state was both hostage to, and manipulator of, competing social groups reveals much about how Pakistan has developed the way it did.

Regardless of how one analyzes Pakistan, it is certain that it was not built upon long-standing political institutions. Pakistan, like Israel, is a country primarily created as a homeland for a religious community that defies the usual rational logic for the establishment of a nation-state. Perhaps not uncoincidentally, the only two religiously founded countries in the modern world, Israel and Pakistan, have both suffered chronic conflict with their neighbors and continuing existential crises about the tolerable boundaries of the underpinning religion (see Devji 2013 for an instructive, if somewhat polemical discussion of the similarities between the two countries). Jaffrelot (2015) has characterized the dilemma as the Pakistan paradox. He writes knowledgeably about the contradictions of Pakistan's lurches back and forth between what he sees as corrupt authoritarian genres of military or civilian leadership. Jaffrelot (2015) sums Pakistan up as three contradictions producing one syndrome. He argues that the multisectoral instability of the country stems from: (1) the tension between the establishment of a centralized nation-state coupled with provinces that were characterized by strong ethnic identities; (2) the competing authoritarian political culture and democratic forces; and (3) competing concepts of Islam (Jaffrelot 2015). Together, he argues these tensions, or contradictions, create the Pakistan Syndrome. The contradictions render the state, in particular, unstable and subject to abrupt and radical change of government. They also offer some evidence to explain why the state and the country it serves do not disintegrate into chaos. In the end, Jaffrelot, like others who have worked in Pakistan, concludes that the state is far from a failure, despite its many weaknesses and instabilities. Unlike some specialists of Pakistan, Jaffrelot offers criticism on all sides of the Pakistan Syndrome. He would appear to have little time for any of Pakistan's leadership regimes and sees on all sides, the seeds of both Pakistan's crippling instability as well as the almost miraculous resilience that allows it to continue apparently always teetering on the brink of Tariq Ali's predicted collapse. Such criticism appears to have mushroomed into something of a cottage industry in Pakistan. Pakistan's intelligentsia are determined to find fault with the leadership on Pakistan. Niaz (2010), for example, blames the state's inability to govern the country effectively on the mentality of its leadership. Using an intriguing framework of historical bureaucratic regimes, Niaz traces what he argues is a decline in the Pakistan state's ability to maintain the autonomous rule of law inherited by the departing British Empire. He develops a tempting argument in which the elite of the Pakistan state increasingly viewed state institutions and the people who work in them as the personal possessions of the leadership. The corrupting influence of that sort of capricious control, he argues, has undermined the development of the rule of law. In the rather provocative closing passages of his book, Niaz concludes that the Pakistani elite have singularly "failed to demonstrate the ability or the will to rise above its own character" (Niaz 2010, 289). He then concludes by saying:

> Due to this failure, it has for all practical purposes condemned itself and the society it presides over to a condition in which the pre-British past and the

post-colonial present and future bear ever greater resemblance to each other. (Niaz 2010, 289–90)

This is not an unusual sentiment to encounter in Pakistan. I long ago lost track of the times I have been shouted down when I've criticized the British Raj and colonialism. While there is undoubtedly some revisionist history involved, there is also some element of empirical validity to *some* aspects of the argument. The British Raj, in the decades prior to its departure, did some things efficiently. A retired police officer who had joined the force immediately after independence, told me of his initial service period under the direct management of a British police commissioner. He was nostalgic for what he perceived was a nearly corruption free police force. To be fair to Niaz, he is not blind to the influence of global politics through the Cold War, and recognizes that a significant cause of Pakistan's problems stem from the ideological tutelage that came from the United States. So perhaps we can infer from Niaz's argument that old fashioned colonialism could come with a degree of responsibility and commitment to the effectiveness of the governance models, whereas the neocolonial replacement was a far more self-serving exercise in brutal *realpolitik*.

Accusations of the culpability of Pakistan's elite have not been restricted to the highest levels of military and government leadership, however. In the rural areas, Martin (2016) rightly exposes the extent to which locally powerful landowners navigate their way around state resources to enrich their own households. Corruption is a tricky concept and while it is arguably uncontroversial to say that corruption is *bad,* it's not always so easy to dismiss some of the strategies for illicit redistribution of state resources as either immoral or unjustifiable. When the "super-elite" pocket billions of rupees, not only might it be understandable for those lower down the food chain to siphon some resources, it might even be considered a moral obligation to do so by some. Martin's ethnographic account of rural landlord political tactics, like this book, demonstrates the extent to which the *local* and the *national* cannot easily be disentangled. Local politics, driven by entirely parochial concerns, cascade up to impact national political parties and actions. Armytage's (2015, 2016) examination of commercial businessmen in Pakistan further suggests that not only are rural power elites principally concerned with parochial self-interest, but so too, are ostensibly more globally connected leaders of enterprise. In a useful analysis of factionalism and class, Armytage unpacks the complex interdependencies, and ultimately impotence, that exist between people who appear to be in control of their own situations. Much as the rural landlords are constrained by values and relationships, urban business leaders are unable to fundamentally shift the power relationships that provide the context in which they operate. Armytage used friendship as the binding rationale for business leaders, but it is clear from her ethnographic accounts that kinship relations are never far from the picture. Rural and urban elites acting in their perceived self-interest, have indelibly shaped Pakistan's electoral landscape. They do so through a variety of mechanisms that draw on their relationships with other people, principally including those people whom they call *kin*. Navigating the turbulent seas of factionalism at the national level, consequently, requires not only effective juggling skills for dealing with competing interests, but critically also pathways for even being given the chance to merge otherwise disparate political networks.

Pakistan's interstitial geographic landscape has been flagged as an inherent source of instability. Kaplan (2012) contrasts an Indus state with a Gangetic state and points to the hydrological divergence of the two major riverine basins of the Indian subcontinent as a partial explanation for why India has so infrequently been united and why modern Pakistan is effectively a rump state that is destined to an unstable and weak future. Whereas stable Indus states from history had successfully linked the Western Gangetic plains with trade routes in Central Asia, the modern Pakistan state is cut off from the vital Delhi plains. This, according to Kaplan, leaves it with only the volatile frontier part of the Indus state of old. While such an analysis is perhaps not as comprehensive as one might like, it touches on an important facet of Pakistan's history. It is the result of multiple partitions and divisions. Despite having a very long history, modern-day Pakistan is made up of effectively new communities of people who did not benefit from the centuries of traditional coexistence and exchange that characterize some other parts of India that are arguably more stable. Whether the isolation from the Western Gangetic tributaries is, in and of itself, a root cause for Pakistan's instability or simply a symptom of more profound issues of dysfunctional relations with India, is perhaps a moot point. The fact remains that Pakistan, despite its hub position between the Middle East, Central Asia, and South Asia, has never been able to capitalize on its geography to establish itself as a key partner in trade between these three major regions of the world.

The intellectual landscape of Pakistan studies is not entirely pessimistic, however. There are those who have marveled at the strengths of Pakistan and have suggested that some of the doom and gloom scenarios over emphasize some of the apparent weaknesses in Pakistan's national identify. If we understand national identity itself as akin to a Barthian symbolic marker of ethnicity (Barth 1969), that is not, in and of itself meaningful, but rather only operates as to differentiate one group from another, then the ambiguity and contradictions of Pakistani nationalism are not necessarily unlike nationalisms that are deemed to be more stable and solid. Hamid (2011) paints a rather optimistic picture of Pakistan's potential future and argues that not only is nationalism over rated as a unifying force underpinning states, but that everywhere nationalism is contested and serves both to divide as well as unite. Although Hamid is a novelist rather than a social scientist, his observations on the tenuous nature of any national identity are well made. Hamid points to the wealth being generated in the country and like many left of center intellectuals, argues that if the Pakistan state could establish a fair tax base across all of its income earning residents, then it would have more than enough resource to deliver all of the public services that would support the middle classes and provide for greater social mobility among the poorest population groups. As of 2011, Hamid says that only 10% of Pakistan's Gross Domestic Product (GDP) was generated from taxation (Hamid 2011, 42). In contrast, Sri Lanka's tax contribution to GDP was 15%, India's 17%, Turkey's 24%, United States' 28%, and Sweden 50%. With relatively modest increases in taxation, the Pakistan state could end its dependence on US aid and, according to Hamid, begin to assume control of its own destiny. It is a bit unfair, and a somewhat unkind, to criticize Hamid's optimism but there are a number of substantial obstacles to the stabilization and strengthening of public services delivery that are unrelated to state resource generation schemes. Some of those are simultaneously sources of stability and strength for the nation of Pakistan, or perhaps more accurately, for the *nations* of Pakistan. For while I agree with Hamid that nationalism is overrated as a *raison d'etre* for any state and there are clear examples of states that function effectively in the absence of agreement on the national identity and character, there are nevertheless clear bonds of loyalty among Pakistani and Pakistani Diaspora populations that work at cross purposes to the goals of the Pakistan state.

Chief among those systems of loyalty and reciprocity is arguably kinship. This is not entirely kinship as one might understand it Western Europe or North America, though it clearly has similarities with how kinship has operated at various times in the history of both of these regions. We need to think about Pakistani kinship as more like aristocratic politicking than a Norman Rockwell painting of ideal family harmony. The network construction and manipulation of Medieval Italian merchant families, perhaps most notoriously evidenced by the success of the Medici family offers a telling, if somewhat romanticized, illustration of the power of kinship as the basis for effective political networking (see Padgett and Ansell 2008 for a good analysis of the role of bridging network connections for consolidating political influence). The delicate politics of kinship in Pakistan is both affective and strategic. It serves to bind people in ways that offer robust stability and remarkable resilience in the face of shocks and crises. Kinship is not the only force that generates bonds of loyalty and reciprocity, of course, but it's one that blends well with a number of other patron-client exchange relationship systems.

IDEA SYSTEMS

Ideas are at the heart of politics. Contestation of control over resources and events is brought about through the production and manipulation of ideas. The beauty of anthropological approaches to ideas is in the ways in which we embed ideas systematically and holistically. In other words, we don't, or shouldn't, isolate ideas from their contexts. They gain their meaning and their utility from their relationship to other ideas, and vice versa. We not only need to contextualize ideas, we need to systematize them—that is, we need to understand them as being the constituent elements of idea *systems*. Systems approaches have been used to good effect across a number of social science disciplines. The fundamental premise of a systems approach is that the sum of the parts doesn't account of the whole. The *interaction* of the parts affects not only the parts themselves, but also the whole. Moreover, systems are the result of interaction and are themselves subject to shock from other systems, so they aren't static, however stable some of them may seem. Kinship is clearly a complex set of phenomena. Some aspects of kinship are clearly identifiable as the expression of idea systems that provide robust replicability across time and space. Those are the core idea systems that allow us to recognize a set of cultural patterns as the *same* even when many of the superficial observed details might be very different.

Acephalous societies offer some intriguing ways of demonstrating the power of idea systems. Nuer politics apparently rested on the interactions between individuals who understood themselves to be connected by kinship of varying degrees (Evans-Pritchard 1940). Gluckman makes explicit the requirement for interconnectedness both *within* Nuer groups and between Nuer and neighboring non-Nuer groups. In the absence of trade agreements or negotiated political treaties, it was the principles of kinship that provided the rudiments of a set of expected behaviors that allowed the Nuer to withstand attacks by Arab traders and British imperialists (Gluckman 1955, 4–7). Rather than simply seeing such acephalous forms of social organization as historical vestiges of a long made obsolete past, it is instructive to look for the ways in which those same principles of organization continue to impact the implementation of formal systems of governance exercised by states—regardless of whether they are formally acknowledged. In Gluckman's original ethnographic studies of Southern African kingdoms, the role of idea systems is subsumed within his greater efforts to establish comparator models of social control (see for example Gluckman 1963, 1965; Gluckman, Mitchell, and Barnes 1949). Thus he focuses on the role of courts and formal authority, rather than adopting the more processual approach favored by his chief opponent at the time, Bohannan (1957), however both Gluckman and Bohannan, in their attempts to understand the control of others, spell out clearly the importance of systems of relatedness and the ways in which people's interactions inform their interpretation of cultural symbols. A generation later, Comaroff and Roberts attempted to draw on the strengths of both the legalistic and processual approaches of Gluckman and Bohannan to develop a coherent account of conflict management that neither privileged, nor neglected, social relations and cultural meanings (Comaroff and Roberts 1981). While their ethnographic descriptions and philosophical contribution is substantial, they didn't draw attention explicitly to the significance of ideational systems that constrain and enable the social-legal processes and the *corpus juris* with which they were principally concerned.

I argue here, as I have argued elsewhere (see especially Fischer et al. 2013) that culture is a complex phenomenon that emerges from ideational systems that are logical and exist prior to any specific expression of them. That's not to say that cultural systems aren't influenced by the things that happen, but the evidence that the underlying cultural systems are subject to high levels of change is somewhat limited. This rather goes against the grain for some social scientist who don't like to see repeated patterns in human behavior and dislike the word system unfairly, in my view. It is not, however, necessary for users of this book to subscribe to the same notion of culture or ideas about the systemic nature of culture to use this book. This influences not only how I interpret data, but perhaps more importantly, what I consider to *be* data and how its constituent elements interact.

ROBUSTNESS AND RESILIENCE IN SYSTEMS

Systems, like people, are reproduced. Unlike people, it's not straightforward to apply Darwinian notions of natural selection to try and make sense of the patterns of societal reproduction and, particularly change over time.[4] Systems are subject to shocks in generation that can result in radical change, including adoption of all or part of other systems. In an analysis of changes in Miskitu kin terminology, for example, English kin terms had clearly been adopted by Miskitu in place of some traditional terms that weren't simply swaps of terms, but introduced structural changes to the way the kinship terminologies related the constituent elements of kin to one another (Jamieson 1998; Lyon, Jamieson, and Fischer 2015). In some ways, the original Miskitu kin terms might be characterized as "broken," but change over time is characteristic of everything. A key feature of a system's ability to both reproduce and adapt lay in the attributes that provide robustness and those that provide resilience.

Read's (2005) careful reading of Rasmussen's data on a Netsilik Inuit community from a period prior to the introduction of hunting rifles, allowed him to illustrate the ways in which critical features of a social system that enable its reproductive success, can introduce unintended brittleness that compromise the system's ability to survive certain kinds of crises. Each adaptation to the system to enable both robust reproduction and resilient response to shock triggered an iterative crisis in the system until finally, the system, as a whole, had evolved to provide a functioning balance of robustness (allowing the system continuity over time) *and* resilience (allowing the system to deal with severe shocks).

CULTURAL SYSTEMS

A great deal of what I deal with here, seeks to treat social phenomena systemically. I treat kinship as the product of cultural systems that are interconnected and impact on one another dynamically. This isn't to say that cultural systems are all one need know to understand Pakistani politics, let alone all human thought and behavior, but rather that cultural systems are foundational to human thought and communication and consequently behavior. They are, to put it a bit crudely, the building blocks not only of the individual (in a social sense) but also of culture and society themselves. This means that I have looked for patterns in the data which can help me to understand the logical systems which shape and inform people's behaviors and their understanding of their own and others' lives.

We do not, as yet, have reliable technologies for reading people's thoughts, so instead social scientists rely on the productions of thought that are expressed in discourse, material culture and behavior. In earlier work I have argued that culture is most usefully understood as the collection of generative information systems that enable effective communication (both spoken and other forms) (Fischer, Read, and Lyon 2005; Lyon 2005). I go somewhat further here and suggest that thought itself, is culturally constrained and bound. So in a very real sense what we might think of as human thought is a cultural production. The tradition emanating from Julian Steward (1955) provided the conceptual inspiration to position cultural systems alongside other systems to better understand people in contexts. The resultant ecosystems models produced following Steward help account for cultural interaction systemically. I don't extend the present analysis to an ambitious total ecosystem, but instead focusing on a critical system, *kinship*, and its immediate impact. By narrowing my scope to deal with a single *foundational* idea system, I provide a robust analysis of how complementary systems of relatedness provide both *robusticity* and *resilience* to Pakistani cultural groups.

ATTACHMENT

Kinship is more than just a set of ideas, however. It provides an observable cultural phenomenon that can be measured and documented, especially in Pakistan where it plays such a prominent role in the everyday lives of people. It provides perhaps the most ubiquitous form of attachment between individuals. It connects households. It provides some measure of predictable reciprocity in an unstable political and economic landscape. In Latour's model of the networks of attachment that bind people and enable agency, the principle that *attaches* people is not be understood as a binary state of presence or absence, but rather of degree. The strength of the attachment, or bind, matters a great deal. Not all attachments are made equal. Perhaps more importantly, rather than a pessimistic view of the constraints that come with attachment, this approach establishes a more generative, productive character to the networks of attachment (e.g., Gomart and Hennion 1999; Lemay-Hébert and Kappler 2016). Freedom, control, power and success are achieved not through *detachment* from constraints but rather *attachments* to productive constraints. Kinship is not, consequently, a constraining network that *impedes* the accomplishment of people's goals, but rather the principle framework of powerful attachments that make those goals possible. The paradox of this scenario will escape no one. So long as kinship forms the primary network of attachments for realizing economic and political agendas, the state of Pakistan struggles to thrive. While the state remains weak, though not failing, it cannot hope to provide households and individuals with the environment of opportunities in which the attachments that shape liberal civil society in Europe and North America has flourished. So as with my earlier work, I cannot condemn systems of inequality and asymmetrical power because to do so would be an act of privileged intellectual arrogance. It is possible to dislike a system and not want to live by its rules without resorting to value judgments about whether that system is right or wrong. The complex network of attachments that create our political and cultural existence make certain things possible and impossible. The role of the useful social scientist is not, therefore to tell audiences what is morally appropriate or inappropriate, but rather to help others *understand* the boundaries of what might be imaginable or feasible within the constraints of the population being described.

Networks of attachment offer a useful conceptual building block in conjunction with other building blocks. By itself it lacks necessary context and just as Latour (1999) suggests, we need to know degrees of attachment and attributes of what is attached. This cannot be an isolated exercise, of course, because the degree of attachment/detachment directly affects the attributes of the network entities. Combining the concept of idea systems with the instantiated relationships they generate, offers a way of understanding the interplay between culture and behavior. Within the domain of kinship in Pakistan, it helps to explain not only why Pakistan has not collapsed, but also why it continues to struggle to survive. The very tools that provide Pakistan its ability to replicate itself across generations and sustain a measure of cultural and societal coherence, are partially responsible for the persistent volatility that undermines the growth of an effective, stable state.

KINSHIP, FAMILY, LINEAGE, AND GROUPS

Anthropology has arguably made more progress in developing coherent theories of some idea systems than others. Kinship, perhaps more than any other single cultural domain, has been explored from the earliest days of anthropology. The consequence of such sustained study, using distinctly varied approaches, has been an accumulation of longitudinal data from geographically distributed locations and communities. This has enabled those anthropologists who specialize in kinship to opt for a genuinely comparative, rigorous set of scientific methods to better develop and refine explanatory and predictive models of kinship as generative idea systems that are foundational to all cultures.

I won't attempt to replicate the excellent summaries of the development of kinship studies within anthropology, nor will I engage in an extended discussion of the strengths and weaknesses of the various approaches to studying kinship. Both of these exercises have been comprehensively and satisfactorily done elsewhere (Stone and King 2019; Parkin 1997, 2004; Holy 1996; Buchler and Selby 1968). Instead, I will provide only a concise summary of the importance of kinship within anthropology and some of the specific work that addresses the conceptual tensions that lay at the intersection of kinship and politics.

From the pioneering days of Morgan (1870), anthropologists have been at the forefront of producing and analyzing data that falls under the broad umbrella term of kinship. This is one of the areas in which it is possible to genuinely see the full breadth of both humanistic and scientific approaches within the discipline. Morgan's interest in the diffusion of cultural ideas was timely (1877). Darwin's (2011 [1859]) contribution to the study of evolution was revolutionizing the study of human societies and a pathway to testing some of the "just-so" folk stories was becoming possible. Morgan's creative development of the use of surveys as a research methodology allowed him to generate comparable systematic datasets on kin terms from Indigenous American groups. While we do not generally subscribe to his diffusionist explanations today,[5] there is no doubt that we owe a debt to his pioneering work in the field of systematic enquiry into knowledge production and organization.

At perhaps the more scientific end of the spectrum, kinship terminologies have been central to a natural science of society. Initially this work focused on classification and the development of typologies for cross cultural comparison, but by the period immediately after World War II, this had given way to a genuine attempt to develop robust theories about the cognitive foundations of kinship systems (e.g., Goodenough 1965; and for a good summary of the shift from classification to more computational forms of analysis see Read 2013). More recent scientific approaches to kinship terminologies have addressed the problems of data production predicated on Rivers' (1900) initial assumptions of the universality of certain core kin terms (Leaf 1972, 2007). In Leaf's elicitation method, there are no *a priori* assumptions about which kin terms are core, but rather these must be established through systematic enquiry. In addition to the development of better ways to produce complete kin term maps, anthropologists have also made considerable progress in building conceptual tools to analyze the cognitive production of the systems. Read, along with collaborators over the years, has developed software to enable researchers to produce kinship algebras capable of generating complete kin term maps from the minimal set of core terms (Read and Behrens 1990; Read, Fischer, and Leaf 2013; Fischer and Read 2005; Read 2006). Mathematical approaches within anthropology may struggle to capture the attention they deserve, but there is no doubt that they firmly place anthropology within a natural sciences tradition of studying society. Anthropologists working in humanistic branches of the discipline have also found kindship central to much of their analyses. Carsten's (1997) work on the creation and maintenance of kinship in a Langkawi Malay community illustrates the centrality of kinship for making sense of how attachments to other people may be socialized in reliable and, importantly, reproducible ways. Carsten uses ethnographic descriptions of the ways in which Langkawi Malay perform kinship and instruct their children in the boundaries of sharing that strengthen or threaten the boundaries of kinship groups.

Over the years, anthropologists have experienced what appear to be crises of faith that all of the preceding work on kinship has been fruitful and represents a truly cumulative effort. Murdock's (1971) Huxley lecture led some to decide that anthropology's fixation with kinship was ultimately spurious. In 1991, when I was a second-year-undergraduate student in a course with the word kinship in the title, our lecturer began the first class by announcing that there wasn't really any purpose to studying kinship anymore. Not only were the societies anthropologists studied more complex and pluralistic, but the entire exercise had proven fraught with serious theoretical and methodological dead ends. He cited Murdock's analysis of anthropology's mythology in the lecture. Needless to say, we then proceeded to study kinship for the full academic year and despite his early assertions to the contrary, he seemed to have spent a great deal of time studying kinship in his own fieldwork.

Verdon (1981) attempted to reconcile the variability of key anthropological kin terms and their associated concepts through a universal, cross culturally salient notion of the group. In his useful analysis of the ideas of kinship, marriage and the family, he spells out the development of two of the principle schools of anthropology: structural-functionalism and structuralism. The emphasis that each of these schools placed on kinship is a useful place to begin analyzing the ethnographic landscape of Pakistani politics. Structural-functionalists, exemplified by the likes of Radcliffe-Brown (1957), understood procreation as one of the goals of kinship. Kin groups, in this model, operate as corporate groups with both role and territorial boundedness. The role of kinship was to establish the boundaries of the group through descent relationships. In this analytical model, the central unit was the "elementary family" composed of parents and children. Structuralism, initiated by the work of Lévi-Strauss (1963), introduced a challenge to this elegant ethnographic model by shifting the focus to the alliances created through marriage. Rather than kinship existing to produce offspring, offspring are in fact necessary for the reproduction of the alliances—the marriages. So structuralism moves from the "elementary family" to the "atom of kinship" which now includes the mother's brother rather than the father.

Pakistani kinship clearly places high importance on both marriage and descent. Rhetorical preference for close cousin marriage results in overlapping descent and marital links between spouses in many cases, but even more significantly, the tensions between resource consolidation and versatile network building mean that Pakistani families must continually maintain strong descent groups that have equally strong ties to other strong descent groups. To isolate a descent group, however strong internally, results in reduced resilience in the face of unexpected shocks. The converse, to dissipate the descent group in search of ever expanding versatile networks, can result in the dissolution and even extinction of the lineage.

Verdon makes an important point about the problems that such variation introduces when carrying out cross-cultural research. The terms kinship, family and lineage are ethnographically salient, but cross culturally contingent not only on local meaning, but also on the analytical assumptions used to generate their representations. Verdon's argument for dealing with such imprecision is to derive a cross culturally valid category of the *group*. Verdon's group attempts to disentangle both interpersonal behavior and normative representations to arrive at something that can genuinely form a conceptual foundation for kinship, family and lineage in ways that are amenable to cross cultural analysis (Verdon 1981). Such operational precision is crucial for cross cultural comparison, but here is less pressing. While it is important to contrast Pakistani kinship, family and lineage with comparable ethnographic examples from elsewhere, the operational need is actually to be able to represent the differing ways that local people invoke the relevant local terms (*rishtidar, biradari, khandan, qaum, jat*). The use of local kin terms is frequent and significant. More importantly, the use of relationships of descent and marriage in addressing crises betrays a profound reliance on kinship, family and lineage as strategic groups. The most appropriate comparisons across cultures, may in fact not be the English terms kinship, family and lineage, but rather some other more strategically defined and manipulated social group that is more intimately connected to politics and economics.

THE ROAD MAP

The second chapter spells out some contextual information about Pakistan.[6] I look at the prevalence of a type of strong man politics in a country that, as I've already suggested, fundamentally destabilizes attempts to consolidate power. As a land of contradictions, Pakistan exhibits a rhetoric of the lone strong leader, but in practice requires continual coalition and cooperation for those leaders to stay in role. Ultimately, the idea of the strong man leader in Pakistan is a barely maintainable fiction that crumbles as soon as key supporters shift their allegiance, regardless of how strong the "strong man" appeared to be. The third chapter offers a historical overview of northwest India, including modern-day Pakistan. In the waves of elite groups that have controlled northern India, one can see clear competitive patterns emerging between caste (*varna*), institutions, kinship (largely lineage, but not exclusively) and various forms of the state (kings, Mughal empire, Sikh kingdom, etc.). Each regime established itself as a "surface" elite that floated along the top of the existing masses while maintaining a distinction from them. The conditions in which kinship has come to play such a prominent role are historical and economic. Successive waves of rule by elite minorities prevented the establishment of a genuine *nation* in which the ruled and the rulers might form a coherent unitary ideal collective. The gap between ruled and rulers alongside the absence of a coherent set of nation building tools, has come to be occupied by alternative networks of resource distribution and social replication. In Hocart's (1950) classic analysis of caste and kinship, caste, kinship and kingship offered parallel and competing institutions of power that functioned to prevent the complete dominance of any institutionalized power network. Over the course of rotating elites in India and what later became Pakistan and Bangladesh, kinship has served to undermine and circumvent both the authority and the legitimacy of the various forms of state that have emerged in the Sub Continent. This both strengthened the importance of kinship, since it provided personal mechanisms for accessing resources beyond the local region, and prevented the state from developing strong institutional forms that might allow for the development of smooth and predictable transitions of power between the rotating groups of elites who were "eligible" to play in the high stakes state power games. British commercial and colonial regimes, like earlier invaders, not only served as "surface" rulers, operating through a complex network of local elites, but also fundamentally destabilized nascent civil-bureaucratic institutions that can be understood as proto versions of state institutions that might have emerged in an independent Pakistan and India.

Chapter 4 shifts to contemporary network creation and maintenance. Without belaboring the subject, I will discuss local terms and concepts that form the foundational notions that we might understand as kinship, which in turn, serves as arguably the most powerful network creation and maintaining idiom. Marriage provides the foundation for the most important political networks in Pakistan. Arranging marriages, including forcing young people to enter into strategically advantageous unions, is a coordinated household exercise. Using both rural and urban data, I examine the processes for arranging appropriate marriage partners. Considerable ethnographic research has been carried out on marriage in Pakistan, particularly in Punjab and Khyber-Pukhtunkhwa, so this chapter combines a review of the existing body of evidence with primary data produced over the course of 20 years of ethnographic research in northern Punjab. The processes used by rural landlords, in particular, illustrates the powerful negotiating strategies inherent in marriages. Such marital networks can reveal a great deal about the motivations and tactics employed by national-level party politicians.

Conflict resides at the heart of all politics. Politics is crucially about managing conflict and the acceptable threshold for different types of political action. The fifth chapter discusses the role of kin groups in managing conflict at local levels. I focus on a particularly turbulent period of local land disputes in a rural part of northern Punjab, in which the participants were effectively under siege in their own village for almost four years. This land dispute is telling because it pitted close cousins against one another and fundamentally re-drew the earlier factional boundaries that I had witnessed in the village in the decade leading up to the dispute. I was able to observe, close up, the collapse of some well-established factions and the painful process of reforming those factions over the four year period. By this point in my relationship with the landlords in this village, I was able to speak directly to older women in the village and learned a great deal more about their involvement in land conflicts. In this chapter, it is possible to identify the role of kinship ideologies in driving some of the justifications used for faction building, but it is clear that kinship alone is insufficient to explain the alliances that emerge.

Since I have audaciously claimed that kinship is key to understanding the continuity and resilience of Pakistan, it is incumbent upon me to bring in the state and party politics. Chapters 6 and 7 examine electoral dynastic political networks and the ways in which the individuals act as representatives of clusters of interests. These dynasties reinforce existing distributions of power and resources. Party politics across South Asia exhibits remarkable evidence of dynastic transmission of authority and control. While there are clearly advantages to restricting potential party leaders in terms of reducing the disruption of leadership contests, this necessarily limits the extent to which parties are able to shift and respond to changes in the political landscape. The Bhuttos are perhaps the most famous contemporary Pakistani political dynasty, but dynastic trends have impacted the shape of Pakistan's provincial and national party politics since independence. In each of these chapters, I look at nationally well-known political families, and try to show their connections to nationally less-well-known, regionally prominent families. One of the characteristics of successful electoral groups is the extent to which they can harness the influence of local networks across different regions of the country to mount effective nationally coordinated campaigns. As with the other chapters, this chapter combines ethnographic evidence from across Pakistan with primary ethnographic material produced in northern and central Punjab to show the ways in which the predictability provided by ascribing charisma and expertise to the offspring of influential leaders can reduce instability while simultaneously retarding the development of effective participatory democratic social institutions.

The final chapter of the book summarizes the principle argument of the book. Kinship is central to all political activity in Pakistan. In traditional Pakistani politics, especially rural landowner politics, descent and marriage connections are transparent and obvious. Alliances and factions are formed using the opportunities created by kin ties. Conflicts are addressed using the same ties, including, at times, arranging marriages to fundamentally change the nature of relationships between rival groups. Kinship networks restrict economic and political choices that are possible for individuals but also provide necessary social support for people in the absence of strong state institutions that might enable the development of stable economic institutions independent from families. At the regional and national levels, party politics are strongly shaped by marital and dynastic networks of relationships that are both reminiscent of landowner politics and intimately connected to them. The rise of ideological politics that hijack religious idioms to challenge the family based oligarchies has served to weaken, but not replace, the long-standing role of kinship in Pakistan. The book concludes by arguing that kinship remains as powerful and central to Pakistani public and private life as ever, but that the rhetorical forms of kinship have morphed into something that may appear more Western and individualistic. However, so long as the state remains incapable of really enabling the development of alternative forms of productive civil society, kinship will continue to serve a primary role in ensuring continuity and stability in the country.

NOTES

1. As Granovetter (1973) demonstrated, sometimes ostensibly weaker ties can be the most politically advantageous because they bridge *across* networks bound with strong ties.

2. Though, of course, they *did* have colonial states in the silent background.

3. I am aware of the paternalistic nuance of calling a group of people "mine." Please know that I do not refer to the people with whom I work as "mine" in any superior sense or with even the slightest hint of proprietary claims over their stories or their lives. I do so out of a bond of loyalty and affection that I hope, and believe, is mutual.

4. In other words, evolution, but note that this should be considered distinct from biological models of evolution.

5. As Bernard (2006) states categorically about Morgan's and others contribution, "The unilineal evolutionary theories they advanced were wrong, but the effort to produce nomothetic theory was *not* wrong" [Emphasis in the original].

6. Throughout the book, where I include direct quotes from my interlocutors, I use pseudonyms to protect their identity. The contexts in which I have carried out my fieldwork have rendered written consent forms not only impractical, but also ethically dubious. Many of the "interviews" I have conducted have been chaotic conversations in which I must periodically remind people that I am a social scientist. Consent, has therefore been established repeatedly through verbal explanation and negotiation. Where I refer to well-known public people, I have used their real names, but at no point did I interact with them directly. All of the information about their genealogical networks has been generated indirectly from public sources such as newspapers, blogs, their own webpages, and so forth.

Chapter 2

Strong Man Politics, Pakistan and Methods

THE DESIRE FOR A STRONG LEADER

Since independence, Pakistan has witnessed a series of strong leaders and their regimes; some scholars have given them credit for reining in the centrifugal forces that would tear the country apart. Lieven (2011), for example, sees a virtue in the strength of Pakistan's military, rural and urban elite leaders who hold chaos and revolution at bay. His description of Pakistan as a "hard country" has clearly irritated many in Pakistan, particularly among the left-wing intelligentsia, but he offers an intriguing defense of the benefits of undemocratic leadership. Such an explanation has the benefit of conforming to commonly heard narratives among military and landowning elites in the country. My own analysis of rural Punjabi landowners (2004) has been categorized along with Lieven's as something akin to an apology for gross inequalities and exploitation (Martin 2016), but that is perhaps too simplistic of a summary of both of our arguments. Both Lieven and I tried to understand arguments that clearly have widespread traction on the ground in Pakistan, but neither of us is blind to the brutality and unfairness of the system in which those folk explanations emerge.

I have sought, elsewhere, to understand the stark reality of a system in which everyone involved seemed to collude with relations of unequal distribution of resources and power even when the distribution clearly favored others more than themselves. I was faced with a seemingly irrational set of actors in a social landscape that made little sense. Why did repeated generations reproduce such systems of cruel hierarchies that materially destroyed those at the very bottom and left those at the top perpetually anxious and insecure? Everyone in between the highest of the elite and the lowest of the powerless poor were left in a perpetual competition to try and both retain what privilege and resource they already possess and, when possible, to raise the status of their household just a bit for the next generation. Make no mistake, retaining status in Pakistan requires skill and dedication. Over the years that I have spent in a small village in northern Punjab, I have been invited to establish my own household. Friends have volunteered to give me a small parcel of land upon which I might build my dream house. We engage in a game of fantasy construction in which we jostle back and forth between my desire for a fairly traditional Punjabi household design that can cope with the heat without the need for economically and environmentally costly air conditioning, and my friend's desire for an architecturally modern house. The conversation always ends the same way. I ask the friend how long he thinks I will be able to retain the house without actually living in Pakistan. He smiles and bobs his head and says that maybe I will have the house for a few months after the construction is complete. They know that an absentee landlord is vulnerable to the growing forces of land mafias and other traditional landlords. The conversations are playful and every friend who has offered me land has assured me that *he* would do what he could to protect my ownership, but *those others* can't be trusted. And of course, they are all right. In effect, no one can be trusted because when one's back is up against the wall, one does what one must to protect one's own family and household.

Therein lay a profound truth about Pakistan. Protection of family and household lay at the heart of so much of what we might disagree with and condemn. To be clear, there are Pakistanis who are as critical of their own society as any foreigners. Pakistanis are not delusional about their own society. Many see its shortcomings and they can definitely attribute causes for them. Those on the left like to blame the military or the rural elite (see, for example, Siddiqa 2007). Those among the rural elite, blame the government. The military often like to blame the civilian political parties (see, for example, Musharraf 2006 for an extended justification of why the military had to assume control). Industrialists spread the blame widely but it includes rural landowners, religious extremists, the military, and political parties. Some brave Pakistanis even include themselves in the list of parties responsible. It's disarming to speak to someone who openly accepts that their unearned privilege is part of the endemic problem of Pakistan's political instability. A casual acquaintance once said to me that it was people like him who exploited the poor and lived a life of luxury who perpetuated the unstable and violent existence that is Pakistan. In his defense, he offered only that this was the system and the only way he could escape his part in it, would be to emigrate to another country. In the end, he said he loved his country and its culture so he opted to remain and live on the "good" end of the system.

THE CONTRADICTIONS OF PAKISTAN

There are clear contradictions between the seeming fragility of the Pakistani state and the country and their refusal to fall apart. The levels of corruption in some quarters are staggering. One of the many interesting things we all learned from the release of the Panama Papers was that the family of the then prime minister, Nawaz Sharif, had somehow managed to invest tens of millions of dollars in somewhat unorthodox and murky investment opportunities around the world. For those at the stratosphere of the global economy, that sum may not seem outrageous, but for those of us rather far outside the top 1%, it's hard to even begin to know *where* such sums might have come from. The sale of properties in Saudi Arabia isn't a particularly satisfying explanation for a variety of reasons that I won't go into here, suffice to say the Supreme Court of Pakistan also found that particular explanation less credible than the Sharifs would have liked. That story is reportedly replicated across many political and civil service families. Pakistan's resources are being siphoned into private hands at a pace that is genuinely difficult to comprehend. At a time when Pakistan's poorest 20% seem to be roughly where they have been for the past 50 years (Jaffrelot 2015), Pakistan's wealthy elite are wealthier and more distant from their fellow citizens than ever before.

Given such instability, then what is it that prevents collapse? Political scientists and economists have done a reasonable job of locating important contradictions in the political culture and systems that might be understood to provide some "ballast" in the turbulent seas of statecraft, but there remain important questions about the actual mechanisms that might create such political and cultural systems at all. Before one gets to *political culture*, one must contend with *culture*. This runs the risk of allowing cynical political players evidence to blame culture as an impediment to progress and change for the better. It may even be an argument with some merit, however, it is not the argument I make here. Rather, this book sets out to identify critical cultural systems that provide continuity and stability to a country that is remarkably *more* stable than it should be. It is not unusual to hear foreigners in Pakistan remark that they feel much safer in the country than they had expected. The negative press around Pakistan belies the reality that most of the time, most people don't encounter terrorist violence, violent crime, corrupt police, or bureaucrats demanding bribes, crooked politicians or brutal and sadistic landlords intent on destroying the lives of their peasants. All of those things exist in the country and to deny them would be absurd, but alongside those clear and indefensible flaws, Pakistan has powerful cultural systems that contain and distribute power in ways that ensure there is sufficient "buy-in" to the state and the idea of Pakistan that it can, and will, persist.

Over the course of my academic career, I have been accused by some of being an apologist for evil landlords. By others, I have been praised for taking the idea of cultural relativism seriously when trying to understand "bad" men. I am often tangential to such argument and watch and listen in awe as colleagues attack one another with gusto and creative reference to an impressive breadth of anthropological arguments. On one occasion, a kind senior academic pulled me to one side and said that it was easy to be lulled into thinking the rural elite were noble and accepting their rhetoric at face value. Perhaps I have done that. Perhaps I still do on occasion. The rhetoric of people afraid of losing privilege can be compelling even while it's possible to step back and see the larger structural injustice of the situation. I am convinced, however, that there are important questions to answer about why so many people collude with relationships of power that manifestly benefit *others* more than *themselves*. Without succumbing to a simplistic Rational Action Theoretical approach, I remain persuaded that people *are* rational and they make what they believe to be the best possible choices in the context. People operate in contexts of imperfect information and they make their decisions within historically and culturally specific domains of moral values systems. So much of what I have written over the past two decades has sought to describe and explain the cultural systems that shape individual people's decision making and participation in complex sociocultural, economic, and political landscapes. I have focused on individual and village level interactions as well as regional and even national-level political players. What I have encountered over the years are genuine forms of cultural continuity that have the power to influence individual people's understanding of evidence, assessment of options and ultimately the choices they make. In Pakistan, by far, the most important cultural system that permeates all others and provides a foundation for all of the cumulative complex systems that emerge is kinship. To be fair, this is really not just a single kinship system, but is itself an aggregate of ideas of kinship relations (terminological systems), gender, hierarchy and reciprocity. Kinship lay at the heart of land distribution, political resource competition, industrial activities, labor organization and is one of the most important obstacles that violent *jihadi* groups must overcome when winning the hearts and minds of young recruits.

To be fair, almost everyone who sets foot in Pakistan has noticed that family matters—*a lot*. So saying that kinship and family are at the heart of important aspects of the political and economic activities of the country is perhaps something of a truism that some might think goes without saying. It must not go without being said, however. We know that kinship and family matter, but we need to know *how* they intersect with other domains and the ways that individuals who are part of those families actively attempt to manipulate and control their *kinship* tools to effect the desired outcomes.

Throughout the book, I strive to balance sufficient background information for those relatively unfamiliar with Pakistan and South Asia without becoming tedious for those who are experts in the region. There are very good histories of Indian subcontinent that do a far better job than I do of providing the detailed explanation for *how* Pakistan came to be and why relations with India are so fraught (see, for example, Talbot 2000; Waseem 1994; Ayaz 2013; Talbot 1998; Metcalf 2004). The role of Islam has provided ample fodder for a productive genre of literature on the country, and the endless debates about the kinds of Islam that have shaped the country are in equal part fascinating and frustrating. The partisan skew of much of what is written about Pakistan means that to get a genuinely objective take on the country is almost certainly an unrealistic ambition. The country faces very real problems and those who care about the country often find it difficult not to take a "side"—even if we can't always manage to stay consistent with the "sides" we've chosen over the years. I can adopt cultural relativism as a powerful theoretical and philosophical tool that enables certain kinds of enquiry and analyses, but ultimately, I am not immune to the distress and suffering that I have witnessed. Despite this, I believe in the utility of a social science that attempts to describe and explain observable and verifiable phenomena rather than simply reflecting a version of the truth. The test of an argument is whether it remains compelling even after the ideological underpinnings have fallen out of fashion. So like those unfashionable anthropological works produced before me that continue to command a grudging respect from those who may disagree with some of the political positions of the authors, I seek to present a persuasive, evidence based case of the fundamental importance of kinship and family systems for key political and economic spheres in Pakistan.

METHODOLOGY

Ethnographies attempt to paint pictures or develop narratives that allow people to better understand a specific group of people. There are many ways that this can be done. Most commonly, it is done using a variety of methods tried out over an extended period of time. In the "good" old days, ethnographers might spend a few years living with a group, learning the local languages and mimicking local patterns of behavior. This part of ethnographic research is what most anthropologists dine out on through their careers. Most of the amusing stories we can tell about our "people" are drawn from everyday experiences of living in a community and learning to de-exoticize them. We learn that however odd or weird we may have found them when we arrived on day one, there is an ordinariness to other communities that becomes evident over time. We develop genuine relationships of affection, jealousy, animosity, and respect. Our embeddedness within other societies and cultures makes some kinds of research more difficult, but opens doors for a plethora of methods that are only possible when there is genuine trust between the people doing the study and the people being studied. The funny stories, however, are only a part of the process. That may be what we use to entice undergraduates into thinking anthropology is a cool discipline, but we merge those with the steady, plodding work of carefully documenting as much of what happens as we can. Many of us also integrate living with people and carefully documenting those experiences with more formal systematic data production using replicable techniques. Sometimes we get lucky and natural experiments fall in our lap, but most of the time, we need to engineer some tasks and ask people to engage in them repeatedly. The first Punjabi village I spent an extended period of time in was probably not expecting the extent of repetition they got from me. I asked over and over similar questions to try and test the limits of my understanding of their lives and culture. Sometimes, they appeared to find the repetition as interesting as I did. Some tasks were less welcome and people have made it clear that while they are prepared to do things to help my research, they don't always like doing it.

Collecting genealogical information from rural Punjabis has been, in my experience, a mutually rewarding experience for everyone involved. They are interested in their family and they know a lot about the kin connections between the people of their lineages. And I found that asking multiple people to help me fill in the gaps of a family genealogy was crucial for ensuring that it was as complete as possible.

Pile sorting, on the other hand, has not proven to be as stimulating for my Punjabi friends as it has been for me. To be fair to them, they've done rather a lot of it for me, but I don't recall anyone coming into my room and asking me to let them sort some cards or photos. The first time I tried a pile sorting exercise, I had several hundred photographs of local villagers and I selected a few dozen that represented a sample from all of the socioeconomic and caste groups resident in the village at the time. Without exception, everyone who did the task resisted rather a lot. They wanted to see the photos and tell me about the genealogical place of the individual and sometimes they volunteered interesting stories about some of the more colorful characters I'd photographed. But they were decidedly uninterested in putting the photos into groups of people that belonged together. The task didn't make sense to them. It made perfect sense to me, but I accept that I did a poor job of explaining it. Consequently, I never made any use of the few results I managed to generate and returned to working with local people on tasks that *they* found worthwhile.

Over the years, I've been able to do more formal data production tasks with local people. I've had them arrange little toy animals in a row to produce data on the distribution of spatial frames of reference. I've had them free list numerous categories of the natural world. I've had them complete surveys that provided household demographic data. Every time, I painstakingly try to explain the purpose of the task and how I intend to use the data. Each time, I'm met with the same bewildered response that goes something like, "I don't care Doctor Sahib. You're my friend and brother. If this is important for your work, then I'll do it." I will always continue to try and explain what I'm doing and on occasion, it's clear that some of the people I work with are sincerely curious and want to know. Most of the time, however, I know that what I'm getting is consent based on friendship and trust, but not usually on a meaningful understanding of the task or the bigger research questions they're designed to try and address.

This book is the result of two decades of data production using mixed methods. Over the years, I have employed interviews, rambling conversations, surveys, free listing, genealogical diagrams, pile sorting, discourse analysis, spatial awareness tasks, map making, social network transactions, social media analysis, direct observation, life history elicitation, ethnographic walks and a healthy dose of participation in the everyday lives of a variety of people across Pakistan. Admittedly, most of this has been done in Punjab and with men. I am proud to have earned the trust of a number of Pakistani women over the years, so while my first book on Pakistan (2004) was almost entirely based on data generated from working with men, I have since been able to build in some experiences and views from a more diverse selection of the population.

The current focus is on kinship. I am necessarily interested in descent and alliance relationships, which means that there will be genealogical data used throughout the argument. I produced this in different ways. One of the wonderful things about kinship in Pakistan is that it is of interest to many people. So I have been able to piece together genealogies of prominent political families relatively easily. Much of the information I needed was publicly available. I discovered that newspaper accounts of politicians frequently include snippets of genealogical information. If a politician has a famous parent, child or in-law, that is often mentioned somewhere in the article. Of course, that didn't give me access to individuals in the genealogy who are uninvolved in politics and are not famous for some other reason. I have respected the privacy of such individuals and even when I have stumbled across their place in the genealogy, I have left them off the diagrams. This is not to suggest that they aren't important, indeed, they may be instrumental for some kinds of communication, but anthropology shouldn't play fast and loose with people's reputations.

PEDIGREES AND SOCIAL NETWORKS

The usual pedigree diagram provides useful information and has the benefit of being familiar to many people in Pakistan. Landowning families are very comfortable producing their own pedigrees or *Shajrah nasb*. Historically these family pedigrees were carefully maintained and monitored by specialists who had cross generational links to specific families. These days, many families are able to maintain their own pedigree records on their own computers. For the so called noble lineages, such as the Syed, descended from Prophet Muhammad's lineage, retaining an accurate and reliable record of one's genealogical history is crucial for establishing one's *bona fides*. I was once having dinner with a wealthy Syed who talked me through the incredible history of his own family's journey from the Arabian Peninsula to South Asia. He knew an amazing amount of detail and had documentation to corroborate every bit of the story. I mentioned another acquaintance of mine who also asserted a Syed lineage. The dinner companion asked a few casual questions about the nature of the evidence proving his lineage and when I said that my acquaintance had told me that his family had lost the lineage documents during Partition, I saw the scorn in the other man's face. He told me casually that real Syeds don't "lose" that sort of documentation. He offered to have the acquaintance's DNA tested for "true" Syed genetic markers, but I never passed on the invitation.

Hull's (2012) insightful examination of a land registry office in Islamabad provides tangible evidence of how important documentation can be. The traditional cloth record of land ownership remains highly prized even though it must certainly be on its way out now that Pakistan has established a functioning National Database Registration Authority (NADRA). The cloth and paper that confirm ownership of land go hand in hand with the *shajrah nasb*. Proving membership in the right segment of a lineage can be the same as proving potential rights to land ownership. It's no wonder, then that landlords fight not only to maintain the borders of their lands, but also the borders of their genealogies.

Genealogical data, however, is insufficient. The interconnected nature of genealogies and resource control mean that while people are certainly interested in policing kinship boundaries, they do so because there are real material consequences to confirming membership within those boundaries. At one level, Pakistanis are quick to invoke kin terms to fast track the feeling of connectedness with others. If I had a dollar for every time a Pakistani called me son, brother or uncle, then I would indeed be a wealthy man. If I had a dollar for every Pakistani who would happily arrange a marriage between me or my male family members with one of his daughters, my retirement fund wouldn't look so rosy. I have earned the privilege of being a very close friend and a kind of brother and uncle in a number of households, but there remains a distinction between that and people who are included in the *shajrah nasb*. I don't take offence at this because it makes perfect sense in the context. To include me would provide no actual benefit to me but would potentially complicate inheritance and land sales for others in ways that aren't worth imagining.

One way of making the materiality of kinship pedigree data more transparent, is to render those same data in social network maps. While there are some obvious limitations to some of the metrics that are applicable when the primary connections are descent and marriage, they nevertheless enable an analysis of the data that is not constrained by *a priori* assumptions about family relations. When those data are layered with data about land inheritance or political party membership, then the intersection of kinship, economics and politics stands out in productive ways.

Rather than spell out the specific methods used throughout the book here, I include as much detail as is necessary to evaluate the validity of the data in the relevant chapters. This discussion is principally driven by a desire to make clear that the arguments presented throughout this book are the result of a long term engagement with many people across many parts of Punjab. My sustained relationships with residents of my "first" Punjabi village are present in this book, but it is not a village study. The *ethnic group* in this case, is not a coherent, homogenous subset of a particular region of Punjab. Instead, I seek to demonstrate what I alluded to in 2004 when I suggested that I had seen some evidence to suggest cultural continuity across northern Pakistan that probably extended to the rest of the country and even across the border into northern India. I will not attempt to integrate India in any meaningful way now, but tackling the extent of cultural continuity across all of Pakistan's regions and social classes *is* one of my main aims.

Chapter 3

Waves of Elites

THE TURBULENT NORTH WEST OF INDIA

I'm not a historian and have clearly not produced a comprehensive historical account of northwest India, including modern-day Pakistan, but it is nevertheless important to try and situate the antecedents that have led to the contemporary political landscape. In the waves of elite groups that have controlled northern India, one can see clear competitive patterns emerging between caste (*varna*), kinship (largely lineage, but not exclusively) and various forms of the state (kings, Mughal empire, Sikh kingdom, and so forth). Each regime established itself as a "surface" elite that floated along the top of the existing masses while maintaining a distinction from them. This both strengthened the importance of kinship, since it provided personal mechanisms for accessing resources beyond the local region, and prevented the state from developing strong institutional forms that might allow for the development of smooth and predictable transitions of power between the rotating groups of elites who were "eligible" to play in the high stakes state power games. I include here the role of the British commercial and colonial regimes who not only served as "surface" rulers, operating through a complex network of local elites, but also fundamentally destabilized nascent civil-bureaucratic institutions that might be understood as proto versions of state institutions that could have emerged in an independent Pakistan and India.

As Sikandar-i-Azam, (*aka* Alexander the Great), approached Taxila, in modern-day northern Punjab, Pakistan, his reputation struck fear in the hearts of local populations. The great and the good of Taxila put their heads together and came up with plan to avert widespread slaughter and destruction. They sent an advance party to meet him well before he neared the edges of the ancient city. They came with a lavish invitation to come to Taxila, to stay as long as he and his army wanted, to eat, drink and be merry as the *guests* of the most hospitable city in the world. Sikandar-i-Azam and his troops arrived in Taxila and were wined and dined and treated to the best of Taxilian hospitality. Sikandar then decided that he didn't need to conquer Taxila. He spared the city and went on his way.

We will probably never know if a word of that story is true, but it's repeated on occasion in and around Taxila both as a signal that hospitality is important to local people and to suggest that they are quick, clever and know how to deal with marauding outsiders. They have certainly had to deal with their fair share of such waves of armed groups passing through the region. The history of the north west of India is a history of conquest. The reins of power pass from group to group and each has left an impact. Local people have both colluded with and resisted such powerful invaders in ways that are a testament to their resilience and ingenuity. As a social scientist who has privileged contemporary over historical data, it's become abundantly clear to me that whether or not ancient Taxilians were astute enough to wine and dine their way out of a slaughter, their modern-day equivalents certainly are. I was told a tale from 1947 in a little village in Attock District, not far from Taxila that illustrates the strategic alliance building that characterizes local social relations. A prominent landowner was "best friends" with the English District Commissioner from Cambellpur (Attock City). The two of them were enjoying a hunting jolly somewhere in the mountains of northern India in the months leading up to independence (before the actual date of independence had been announced). The landowner's 17 year old son, meanwhile, was languishing in Campbellpur jail for 17 days for participating in protests against the British colonial rule. I am definitely too young to have known that jail when it was called Campbellpur, but I am well aware of how brutal and dehumanizing Attock City jail was supposed to have been, so I think it's fair to say that the son had to be committed to the cause to endure such hardship. When I was told this story, by the son, who was an elderly landlord by the time I met him, I asked, naively, what his father thought about him protesting against his father's "best friend."

He answered casually, "The British were good people. They gave us many good things. But it was time for them to go. They had to leave. It was our country and they had to go, but they weren't bad people. My father didn't mind what I did."

Therein lay a cognitive skill that I've witnessed time and time again in Pakistan that I have admired and envied since the first time I encountered it. At first, I wondered how generous a person had to be to acknowledge the goodness of their political enemies. Where did such wisdom and maturity come from? Over the years, as I've learned more about the history of both the country and people's lived experiences, I have come to realize that such an enlightened attitude is not unusual and is not correlated with higher education or literacy, but is very much a part of the way many ordinary people view those around them. Being political enemies does not preclude respect and even, on occasion, affection.

In 1983, following the Sabra and Shatila massacres in Beirut, I wandered into the center of Lahore wearing a baseball cap that said US Army, wearing shorts, flip flops and a t-shirt. I was a teenager who couldn't imagine his own mortality and wasn't aware of how my attire might impact the way other people perceived or judged me. There were apparently more than 100,000 protesters demanding justice and calling for Israelis and Americans to pay for the slaughter of innocent Muslim men, women and children. I later heard that there were more than 14,000 volunteers to go be martyrs in Palestine/Israel. I asked the people around me what was going on. Complete strangers patiently explained that innocent Muslims, including children, had been murdered by the Israelis and the American government let them do it. I know now that it was slightly more complicated than that, but I had no reason to doubt them at the time and was suitably horrified. Regardless of the details they got wrong, the massacre was inexcusable and horrific. It's one of the low points in 20th century history. I expressed my horror and sympathy and asked what could be done. At no point throughout the event did anyone show me anything other than kindness and patience. I expect that today I wouldn't receive such a generous reception and there are a number of reasons for why that almost miraculous separation of individuals from their governments and states has been eroded. At the heart of the reasons for such a clear separation is something that emerges from the political nature of kinship organization in the country.

A HISTORY OF ROAMING MARAUDERS

The borders of modern-day Pakistan have been crossed by numerous armies. The legendary visit from Sikandar-i-Azam is only one of many stories that local people have about invading hordes. Some of the soldiers settled in the area and became part of the local mix of people. Others passed through and left little to no impact. One of the most prominent *qaum* (lineage descent group akin to a nation) claims direct descent from the men who travelled with Mahmud of Ghazni, who led one of the most important Muslim conquests of northern India around the year 1000 (Schimmel 1982). Such descent claims hint of the history of invasions. The lineages, the origin myths, the marriage preferences all reflect something of the past. The hardships and the alliances that have formed over generations are evident in the contemporary family landscape.

The Khattar *qaum* claim a link to the Abbasi, or descendants of the paternal uncle of the Prophet Mohammad (Lyon 2004, 132–33). Those groups that claim no local descent, and consequently no Hindu past, do so through careful insistence on their genealogies and an insistence on their non-South Asian origins. There are those who invoke a fairly direct connection to the Prophet via his daughter, Fatima, and son-in-law, Ali ibn Abi Talib (Imam Ali), who was also his patrilateral cousin. Syeds, as they are known throughout the Muslim world, hold a special place in Islam. They are not a priestly class, nor do they necessarily hold positions of significance or power in society, but they are nevertheless afforded respect as a consequence of their family tree.

Other prestigious *qaum* adopt similar tactics of either *ashraf* (noble, usually Arab) origins, or purity of lineage even if the South Asian origins cannot be denied, such as Rajput or Jat. Descent alliance figures prominently in the rationale behind political alliances and the historical accounts of resistance to invading armies, or the basis upon which successful invaders have organized their support have been able to assert a kinship organizational foundation with few challenges.

These so-called tribal politics have reportedly had a profound impact on the organization of kinship across northwestern India/Pakistan. Ahmed and Barth both described the importance of patrilateral kin groups for regional political negotiations (Ahmed 1976; Barth 1959). Their recognition, however, was not a simplistic application of anthropological assumptions derived in Sub Saharan Africa, but rather served as a challenge. The bloc alliances of the Swat Valley of Pakistan, they argued, represents a divergent case in which patrilineal descent is of prominent importance for politics, yet did not develop into larger lineage corporate groups (Ahmed 1976, 40; Barth 1959, 5). Ethnographic evidence from beyond Pakistan suggests that alliance blocs that coalesce around patrilineal descent groups may represent considerably more complex political and economic phenomena. Among Kazakh pastoralists, Arghynbaev (1984) has argued that while the rhetorical bonds of mutual obligation are rooted in historical kinship, the accumulation of resources, especially cattle, means that Kazakh pastoral factional alliances must be understood as class relations. Even taking into account the Soviet influence on Arghynbaev's analysis, there seems a strong ethnographic case that descent kinship across Central Asia (extending into the northern part of modern-day Pakistan) is a vehicle for political alliance formation, but not one that can or should be understood in terms of the rhetoric of family espoused by local people. Extending this point, it seems clear that descent alone can never provide the necessary systemic robustness that would allow a political bloc to survive over time. One mechanism for introducing resilience into these potentially rigid patrilateral blocs was apparently creative forms of fostering by way of milk kinship (Parkes 2005). The use of suckling to create bonds of kinship seems to have existed historically beyond the Muslim world (Parkes 2004), but even today continues to play some marginal role in generating meaningful kinship ties that address cultural obstacles to satisfying basic domestic requirements. There appears to be some persistent strategic role for milk kinship in contemporary Qatar for creating relationship bonds that allow men and women to interact while still maintaining strong *purdah* boundaries (El Guindi and al-Othman 2013). These fascinating creative tactics for building bridges across patrilateral descent blocs remain relatively trivial in number, however, so while they provide a tantalizing example of innovative human navigation of ostensibly incompatible cultural structures and pragmatic solutions, they do not offer a credible explanation for the empirical reality of political alliances in Pakistan. Bloc alliances appear to have depended, instead, on the resilience provided by marital alliances that serve competing purposes, including binding blocs nominally based on descent.

THE MUSLIM ERA: MUGHAL AND SURI EMPIRES

One of the most successful invasions of South Asia is certainly that of the descendants of Timur (Tamerlane) and Chingiz (Ghengis) Khan, the Mughals. The first Mughal emperor, Zahir al-Din Muhammad Babur, was expanding from a position of weakness following the ouster of his Timurid-Chaghatay Mongol kingdom from their historical homeland of Mawarannahr (Transoxiana) in Central Asia. His defeat of the Afghan king at Panipat in 1526 heralded the start of two centuries of Mughal control over the northern part of India. Marital alliances were hugely important for the Mughal empire. Marriage was one of the principle mechanisms for creating alliances across political oppositional blocs. Balabanlilar's (2012) historical account of the Mughal empire, in fact, begins with a genealogy that first introduces each emperor and a list of their spouses and the children from each marriage. More importantly, in her account of the defeat at the hands of the Uzbek invaders from the east, she writes of the use of rape to terrorize the defeated populations and forced marriage to establish legitimate claims to political ascendancy (Balabanlilar 2012, 18–24). These marriage practices associated with Uzbek and Mughal ruling elites, in fact, mirror those of more recent landowning elites seeking to establish legitimate claims to ownership and control. Marriage, it would seem, has long been a pathway to legitimation through the benefits of descent membership it offers to the offspring. The use of marriage for legitimizing descent claims to ownership is an interesting example of the implicit contradictions in dominant explanations of conception which hold that mothers do not transmit substance to their offspring, but only provide a nurturing vessel that supports and enables the substance (*nasl*) of the father (see Lyon 2017). In addition to the possibly contested descent claims that come from entering into extended marital alliances with enemies whose claim to rule and own a territory may be the simple creation of alliances. While it would be naïve to infer that sibling affection would create tangible political alliances across competing political blocs all by themselves, as part of other strategic initiatives, they appear to have been pivotal at certain times in South Asia's political history—and this is particularly evident among some of the Mughal emperors.

Marriages form legitimate alliances between households, but concubinage also may have played a role in consolidating Mughal control over some parts of India that were resistant to forceful takeover. Dheer (2016) claims that the most unifying of all Mughal emperors, Akbar, had 30 wives and more than 6000 concubines, and while it's unclear how such a harem might genuinely have served to strengthen his political network of allied states, network building appears to have been at least partially the motivation.

The Mughals did not enjoy uncontested hold over the reins of power throughout their era. Sher Shah Suri, a soldier in the Mughal Emperor Babur's army, was able to force out Humayun, Babur's son to establish the short lived, but influential Suri Empire. Sher Shah Suri and his son, Islam Shah Suri, ruled for a relatively brief period of time (1540–1556), but developed administrative state structures such as a postal service, expanded the transportation network across north India, issued the first standard currency, and set up a more easily administered, modern system of taxation. The reformations introduced by Sher Shah Suri were to prove instrumental for the Mughal Emperor Akbar, when he finally managed to re-establish the Mughal Empire in 1556.

THE SIKH EMPIRE

The Sikh Empire was effectively a one generation phenomenon. Maharaja (King) Ranjit Singh successfully took control of an area that roughly corresponds to modern-day united Punjab (that is, both the Indian and Pakistani Punjabs). His widow and son held on for a few years after his death, but fundamentally, the Sikh Empire lacked the ability to transition to a new leader. During Ranjit Singh's time, Punjab underwent considerable turbulence. The British did not idly accept a Sikh Empire on the border of the territory they were increasingly looking to control. The British had politically neutered the last Mughal Emperor, Bahadur Shah Zafar, and were busying themselves with direct and indirect attempts to undermine Sikh control over the Punjab. One of the ways that they were able to ensure that Punjab did not unite under a Punjabi king, was the promise of land gifts in exchange for support. Across

Punjab there were a number of prominent families that benefited substantially from the fall of the Sikh kingdom. Sir Sikandar Hayat, a very famous Khattar from northern Punjab, as well as an eminently respected Muslim leader of 19th century India, famously supported the British and he and his family were handsomely rewarded. Across Punjab similar stories meant that despite reigning for half a century (1799–1849), the Sikh Empire was neither peaceful nor uncontested.

The march of invading armies through some parts of Punjab remained a powerful myth as recently as the late 1990s. In my earlier work on a village in Attock District, I wrote of the relocation of the village from a convenient spot in between two small mountains to the top of one of the mountains (Lyon 2004). I was told that this was a result of Ranjit Singh's marauding armies who used to pass through the area on their way between fighting the Afghans to the west and the British and Hindus to the east.

One of the most important local shrines in the area may also owe part of its origins to the chaos created by the passing armies at this time, although the literal truth of the origin story must be understood as only partially informed by actual historical events. The saint at the top of the little mountain on the outskirts of Bhalot village in Attock District, is said to the burial spot of a prominent Gujar saint, or *pir,* named Baba Shaikh Daud[1]. Baba-ji, as he is sometimes affectionately called, has an elaborate tomb and surrounding his grave, are the graves of some of his family. The people of the village have run electricity to the top of the mountain to provide light for Baba-ji at considerable expense. Since my first visit there in 1998, the grave has gone from a relatively modest open gravesite, to an enclosed shrine with a domed roof. The old footpath has been paved and stairs have been added to ease the walk. A metaled road to the top provides access for older people who struggle to walk, as well as some younger people who find themselves in a rush but still want to pay their respects to Baba-ji prior to taking on onerous tasks or dealing with dangerous responsibilities. The origin story is a fascinating for a number of reasons[2]. Firstly, it reveals the rich syncretism of Punjabi Islamic practice and belief. The imagery and symbolism, along with the ritual activities, are more than a little suggestive of pre-Islamic foundations in the region. As the story goes, Baba Shaikh Daud's sister, whose name appears not to have been retained through the passage of time, was in Bhalot and two rival groups of men were arriving to claim her as their bride. At the time, her family, the ancestors of the current dominant landowning family, were not able to defend her against two groups of armed men. She climbed to near the top of the small mountain and prayed to Allah to please save her from being taken against her will. The mountain then opened up and she was able to escape by entering the newly created tunnel. The opening close behind her, trapping her shawl (*chador*) which, to this day, some people claim to see flapping on the side of the mountain at particular times of the year. Elsewhere, I've argued that this origin story owes at least part of its narrative to stories contained in the Rig Vedas, which talk of the purity and strength of the love between a brother and a sister and how the love of the sister, in the Hindu context, conferred godhood on the brother (Lyon 2017). In the context of Bhalot, there is no suggestion that Baba Shaikh Daud became a god, but rather that he became a spiritually noble and powerful person. In the many years that I have visited Baba Shaikh Daud's shrine and spoken to people about the origin of the shrine and about the importance of the shrine today, I have never heard any explanation for the origins of Baba Shaikh Daud's spiritual power other than this. Subsequently, he has demonstrated his power, or at least influence, many times over. Indeed, I was advised to ask him for help on one occasion in 1999 and I can confirm that my problem was resolved in a very satisfying and timely manner following my conversation with Baba-ji. The significance of this shrine here, however, is slightly different. The timing of the life of Baba Shaikh Daud is somewhat murky, but there seems to be some preponderance of opinion that would suggest he lived during the time of Ranjit Singh's Punjabi kingdom. Rather amazingly, almost 200 years after the fact, the community of Bhalot were still being reminded of the danger and instability of this time period through tales of the relocation of their village and in the origin story of an important local saint.

Persistent instability and anxiety about invasion and attack were apparently a fact of life for many parts of Punjab. At high political levels, armies marched through Punjab on their way to Delhi, Peshawar, Kabul, Lahore and beyond. The prizes may have been the big cities in the plains or the mountain capitals, but everywhere along the way felt the pain of loss and insecurity. The consequence of this was to make lineage groups a principle source of succor and security. Kinship groups, which had long served as an important social institution for the organization of labor in agricultural villages, assumed greater importance as distant villages became encompassed in empires that were as brutal as they were capricious and unstable. The moments of relative harmony and reasonably smooth bureaucratic order were undone by alternative regimes with visions for change.

THE BRITISH RAJ

I have heard a number of Pakistanis express degrees of nostalgia when talking about the British Raj. It's a curious phenomenon because arguably, the evidence is fairly compelling that the benefits of the Raj were driven by what profited Britain. Tharoor (2017) makes a compelling case for the causal relationship between the *deindustrialization* of India and the *industrialization* of Britain. This isn't to deny that the British did things that benefited some people in India, but that doesn't appear to have been their motive. The caste system, for example, was firmly in place prior to the arrival of the British (or the Mughals), but the British were apparently entirely willing to stoke communitarian and sectarian animosity in order to concentrate their own hold over the subcontinent. When the British finally consolidated their control over northern India, including modern-day Pakistan, they did so with a bureaucratic sophistication that had not been seen in earlier regimes that allowed them to exploit local production more efficiently than their predecessors. The Mughals and the Sikhs, to be sure, had administrative agents who collected taxes and provided some degree of a uniform "rule of law," but the erratic policy changes that could be triggered both during and between rulers meant that for the most part villages were not meaningfully incorporated into something approximating the Westphalian style nation-state. To be sure, nor were the British able to establish anything approaching a coherent nation-state, but then, that was never their aim. Arguably more than any previous ruling elite, the British were more blatantly in it for themselves. The British Raj's model of governance may have been the most crassly exploitative of any regime in India. The separation of ruling elite and ruled masses was hardly new to India, but it was perhaps more strikingly clear. The Mughal, Suri, and Sikh empires were, for better or worse, clearly *of* India, despite their minority faith. In the case of the Mughal and Suri empires, the faith was also of foreign origin. The British, in contrast, stood apart from all Indians and the colonial state even apparently viewed the descendants of Anglo-Indian marriages with some suspicion. Tharoor (2017) is undoubtedly correct in his dismissal of the rose tinted version of history that portrays the British as the "enlightened despots," to use Tharoor's description, who brought infrastructural and governance sophistication to the country.

The British, like the regimes that came before, struggled to fully incorporate all rural areas, nor did they particularly seem to want to do that entirely. It suited the British, as it suited their predecessors, to retain buffer regions between their own centers of power and those of their rivals, particularly the Afghans. When thinking about the British Raj, it is critical to distinguish between those places they attempted to control, such as Lahore, Delhi, Mumbai and Kolkata and the peripheral areas in which they seemed content with a rather more light touch rule, such as Rawalpindi Division. The garrison town of Rawalpindi had a prominent military presence, but lacked the development in the arts and diverse commercial and industrial activities that were found in the heart of the British Raj.

The British, like their predecessors, did not have a tranquil regime. Throughout the British Raj, both before and after the 1857 Mutiny/First War for Independence, Britain faced resistance to its control over India.

The morally questionable genius of the British was to use existing fractures in Indian society to destabilize the most dangerous opposition. When the Mughal puppet proved less controllable than anticipated, the British actively suppressed Muslim unity and political mobilization through currying favor with some Muslims, who renounced any aspirations for a return to Muslim rule over India, in exchange for land and privilege. With Hindus, the British cultivated the educated classes and provided pathways to wealth through the civil service and as political agents. The term "divide and rule" is so frequently heard in Pakistan today, specifically in relation to the British, that it begins to sound like an implausible conspiracy theory. Can the British really have been so forward thinking and devious that they were able to play Hindu, Sikh and Muslim against one another? It would be nice to be able to lay the blame at the feet of the British if for no other reason than if it were really possible for them to have engineered these divisions, then it might be easier to imagine a way to engineer their eradication. Sadly, the reality is not so convenient. The British undoubtedly harnessed existing tensions and in certain times and places were able to exaggerate and trigger tensions to suit their purposes, but they did not invent resentment between communities. The divisions between religious communities in India have been brewing for a very long time and are the consequence of invasions, subordination, discrimination, exclusion and violence. The success of the British may not principally have been because they were masters at managing these tensions, but because for much of the time they were in control of India, they were outsiders who were able to remain outside the "real" disputes. As outsiders, in addition to not being the prime focus for animosity, they also benefited from the obligations of hospitality that continue, on occasion, to supersede political opposition.

The 17 year old young man who spent time in Campbellpur Jail, while his father was enjoying a hunting trip with the British District Commissioner, was clear that the British were good people, but their time had come. They had to leave when they did. Pakistan and India needed to be led by people from the Sub Continent. The two nation solution that ultimately emerged in South Asia, didn't compel, or even allow, the reconciliation of longstanding animosities, but instead enabled them to calcify and become even more immutable than anyone might have imagined prior to independence. That young landlord's son fought a political battle with the group of people with whom his father had forged strong political alliances. They had adopted a tactic for dealing with the overwhelming power of an enemy that maximized the security and continued status of their household. It relied on kinship in ways that do not neatly conform to traditional anthropological theories of patrilineal agnatic segmentary oppositions. In that tidy theory, one expects brothers against cousins: first patricousins against more distant and matricousins: all cousins against non-cousins and so forth. In the face of complex, interconnected empires, kingdoms and colonial bureaucracies, however, such simplistic opposition is easily crushed unless there is an overwhelmingly treacherous physical environment on one's side. Northern Punjab may be semi-arid and have some small mountains, but there was nothing to protect the many agricultural communities in the area had they chosen to try to unite in opposition to the Mughals, the Sikhs or the British. Instead, they formed contradictory alliances and relationships in which the "winner" of any particular political struggle was the "friend" of someone in the kinship group. To be sure, this didn't mean that everyone liked, trusted or even tolerated everyone else in their own kinship group (quite the opposite in many cases), but the bonds of kin obligation are not dyadic or short term. They are dependent on multiple layers of connectivity and persist over time. Kinship in Pakistan (and India) is a long game and it's maintained both consciously and unconsciously through easy to replicate cultural rituals and patterns that make it extraordinarily difficult to challenge or change.

PARTITION AND *MOHAJIRS*

The independence of India and Pakistan marks a significant change, in some ways, from earlier forms of instability and uncertainty. While the Pakistan state has been decidedly unstable since it was formed, there are reasons to argue that the establishment of a Pakistani "nation," in the sense that Gellner (1983) meant, has not been, at least partially, successful. Pakistan has developed a functioning civil service that in many respects is an exemplar in meritocracy, even if it does not always appear fit for purpose (if the purpose is what one expects from the particular branch of the civil service). The two major areas in which the Pakistan state has failed to live up to its promise as a modern bureaucratic entity, is in the extent to which the electoral class is unable to effect profound change and the willingness of the military to intervene, both overtly by declaring martial law, and covertly by preventing elected officials from taking any action that might threaten military dominance over political life. I write this with profound respect for both the elected officials and the military personnel because the more I have known the men and women who assume these roles, the more I understand that the forces that constrain them to act in the ways that they act are neither trivial nor easily understood. This is not to exonerate them, but rather to be brutally honest and admit that there but for the Grace of God, go I. It would take a truly exceptional individual, with almost super human powers of persuasion and charisma, to radically challenge the direction of travel that Pakistan has been enduring for the better part of 70 years.

So rather than heap condemnation on the political and military elite for perpetuating instability, uncertainty and capriciousness in Pakistan, I want to shed light on *why* it's so challenging for *anyone* to bring about change. As I have argued before, the very institutions that allow Pakistan to survive and enjoy continuity and security at local levels, are the root of why it is a Herculean task to effect significant change in models of governance.

It would be completely wrong factually, morally and politically to describe the post-independence migration of Muslims from modern-day India as an invasion. It was not. It was, however, an incredible flux of people that fundamentally changed the population of Pakistan. Some parts of Pakistan were relatively less affected, but no place was immune from the ramifications of millions of people flowing across the newly created border. These migrants, called *mohajir* (migrant), have had a major impact on the political, economic and cultural landscape of the country. One of the most popular political parties in Sindh, MQM, was formed around the idea that *mohajir* have a unique set of political and cultural experiences that had not been adequately represented in electoral politics. Initially, MQM stood for Mohajir Qaumi Movement, but there have been a number of factional splits and the dominant group now refer to themselves as Muttahida Qaumi Movement.[3] The direct impact of migrants from India is felt keenly in the canal colonies of Punjab, and some of the major cities, especially Karachi. The movement of people from the Partition of Pakistan and India continued for several years after independence as a result of ongoing violence, intimidation and discrimination against the minority communities. Many of the migrants were reluctant and bitterly regretted having to change countries. The famous writer, Saadat Hasan Manto, by all accounts, had no desire to leave his beloved Bombay/Mumbai, but found himself unable to work in the film industry. His move to Pakistan would prove to be uncomfortable both for him and for the Pakistan state, which was troubled by some of his graphically provocative stories. His short stories about the horrors of Partition are particularly poignant reminders that the Indian subcontinent's independence came at an extremely high price (Manto 2001). The trauma of the violence, like the trauma of earlier invasions, has left a legacy in the country today that has rendered the state a suspect and uncertain category. It should come as no surprise in the wake of such experiences that people turn to social and cultural institutions that have proven their resilience and value over time.

ELITE DIFFERENCE AND CHECKING POWER

The singular pattern that stands out throughout the history of South Asian ruling elites is their *distance* from the people they ruled. The Mughal rulers came from Central Asia and ruled a Hindu majority. When the Sikhs, who claim Punjabi indigeneity, rose to supremacy, they were a religious minority dominating ethnically close, but religiously distinct populations. The British were complete outsiders, religiously and ethnically. In the immediate aftermath of the creation of Pakistan, the ruling elite came from the Indian Muslim League, a party that was dominated by Indian Muslims from Dhaka and Mumbai—not the major cities of contemporary Pakistan. Since 1947, the founding year of Pakistan and an independent India, the country has had repeated bouts of military rule. Two of the three most significant of ruling generals (Ayub Khan, Zia ul Haq and Musharraf) were themselves Urdu speaking *mohajirs* who had migrated to Pakistan from other parts of India (Zia ul Haq and Musharraf).

The gulf between the ruled and rulers is replicated across the country. In Attock District, the dominant landlord family are members of the Khattar *qaum,* while the majority of peasant farmers are either Gujar or Awan. In the few Gujar dominated villages, a high majority of the peasant farmers are from the Awan *qaum.* There are many consequences of the pervasive model of rule by something other than "the people," but one is the generation of clear conceptual boundaries between rulers and ruled. Unlike experimental democracies, such as the United States, in which citizens are repeatedly taught to identify with the state as an extension of "the people," there is no such exhortation in Pakistan. The people are *not* the leadership. The leadership is composed of a separate and distinct elite who maintain their status and control through careful negotiation of competing interests. The elite have never been, and certainly are not today, unified around their shared class interests, except in the loosest possible sense. Instead, they exhibit every sign of being highly fractious and competitive. The mechanisms for ensuring no single elite network manages to cling to power for too long, or enjoy absolute power at any time, are complex and partly revolve around the dynamics of kinship that, for all its flaws, has proven quasi irrepressible and therefore an ideal tool for checking the power and authority of formal economic and state institutions.

In the next chapter, I turn my attention to the basic tools of kinship—creating networks through marriage and descent. While this may seem far removed from the stuff of empires and global nation-state politics, these networks form the bedrock upon which the Great Games depend. Without kinship networks, the party political affiliations would lack coherence and strength. I appreciate that some may object to leaping back and forth between villages and national political organizations, but critically, the same mechanisms appear to provide the wiggle room for individuals and groups to cope with extreme shocks. To be sure, I'm not suggesting that these systemic resilience points are a formula for an equitable or fair system of resource redistribution or political representation, but rather that they make a harsh context viable for more people.

NOTES

1. The name itself is informative. Baba=old man, Shaikh=holy or spiritually important. Daud is the Muslim equivalent of David. So the name literally means Holy Old Man David.

2. I discussed the significance of the origin story elsewhere to illustrate the significance of cross-sibling relations in South Asia (Lyon 2017).

3. In 1997, the party replaced the word *Mohajir* (migrant) with *Muttahida* (united). Despite the name change, the party's appeal remains strongest with Urdu speakers who are the descendants of migrants from India.

Chapter 4

Descent, Marriage, and Building Networks

"We Pakistani people, we don't love our wives when we marry them. We learn to love our wives after 10 years of being married." A Punjabi landlord in 1999.

"My father was a wise man, but on this topic he was wrong. We never learn to love our wives. After 10 years, we understand our wives." The landlord's adult son in 2014.

DESCENT AND ALLIANCE

The shift from focusing on descent to alliance was a major breakthrough in social anthropology. It wasn't that marriage was unimportant, but the attention, particularly of British social anthropologists working in sub-Saharan Africa seems to have been disproportionately aimed toward the rhetoric of paternal relations. Descent groups offered a powerful idiom of political organization that seemed to be used to justify and regulate resource distribution, marriage prohibitions, inheritance, and political action. The development of segmentary lineage theory seemed to provide a coherent explanation for much of the observable political activity for groups like the Nuer (Evans-Pritchard 1940), the Tallensi (Fortes 1949), or the Tiv (Bohannan 1958). Sahlins (1961) aptly noted the predatory nature of the concept of segmentary lineage in anthropology at the time. He argued that while the notion of segmentary lineage might be useful for some societies, it was a poor fit in many ethnographic cases. In Pakistan, like most of the Middle East, emphasizing lineage descent has the benefit of fitting a particularly salient rhetorical idiom on the ground. People frequently talk about concepts like *nasl* (breed or pedigree) that shape the individual. Patrilineal descent is highly relevant for establishing one's social position and determining inheritance. While it is true that Islamic law mandates inheritance to female offspring, the custom in most of Pakistan appears to have excluded daughters from inheriting immovable assets until relatively recently. Widespread notions of conception would tend to reinforce an emphasis on descent. Even though Pakistani schools teach biology, for the most part, more or less the way it is taught in Britain or the United States, people continue to invoke the idea that the mother is a "vessel" into which the father pours his essence to make the baby. Any anthropologist encountering such a notion of conception might be forgiven for not considering marriage as prominent or important as descent. The reality is both more interesting and more problematic. Marriage is a major preoccupation for Pakistanis. It is a life altering event that entitles individuals to a step change in social identity, as well as nominally shifting the rights and responsibilities applied to individuals.

This chapter is all about the complementary types of relatedness in Pakistani kinship systems: marriage and descent. Descent provides the "hard" bonds that are ostensibly irrevocable and help to unify groups. Marriage serves to build bridges between otherwise isolated descent groups. Both forms of relatedness are conceptual and require cultural systems to give them form and power, however much the cultural language used to describe them may be rooted in ideas of primordiality or immutability. I start with a manifesto of sorts declaring not only that kinship is *important* in Pakistani societies, but that it serves as critical foundation upon which the rest of society depends. That is not to say it's the *first* social institution[1], but that it is pervasive and gives meaning and structure to so many other social institutions that to extract it would prove fatal for all other social and cultural organizations and practices. I then discuss descent relatedness in both rural and urban Pakistan to illustrate its prominence and cultural salience on the ground. Following this, I tackle the idiom of patrilineality and show that despite a strong tendency to downplay the significance of maternal transmission, there is a long tradition of recognizing matrilineal substance inheritance in Punjab. Few, if any Pakistanis, would deny that Mothers matter a great deal, but they frequently invoke notions of maternal care that are rooted principally in the direct transactions between mothers and their offspring. In fact, mothers matter in the same way that fathers matter—because their lineage and corporate histories and interests are introduced into the household and influence every member of the local kin group. This influence is, of course, related to the network connections generated by the marriage unions as well as conceptual ideas about maternal transmission. In order to appreciate the extent to which marriages matter, it helps to spend time with Pakistani kinship terminology, so after dismantling unilineal descent propositions, I briefly describe the rich Urdu affinal kin terms. These suggest that unlike in English or American kinship terminology, marriage is a way of creating *real* kinship that is as rudimentary and solid as descent based relatedness. Even if marriages can and do end in divorce, they establish relationships that can have long lasting repercussions for everyone involved. In the examples given in the chapters on conflict management and electoral politics, it becomes clear that while divorce does indeed bring about important changes in relations, the points of connection through the resultant offspring from any unions remain powerful bridges for mobilization and action.

THE BACKBONE OF SOCIETY

It's no accident that anthropologists from Morgan onward paid attention to kinship. What they study varies, but it is one of the characteristics of human groups. It may not actually set them apart from *all* other mammals, especially some of the great ape species, but it clearly provides a powerful idiom for defining who *we* are to ourselves. As with a few other domains within cultural anthropology, the extent to which it should even be considered distinct is questionable. Comaroff and Roberts (1981) posed the question of whether *legal* anthropology wasn't, in fact, just *anthropology*. What legal anthropologists study, after all, are fundamental issues of social control, resource distribution, and conflict management. Kinship, interestingly is not defined in the same way as legal anthropology (i.e., nobody defines themselves as a *kinship anthropologist*), but like legal anthropology, kinship cross cuts every other domain of the social and cultural lives of people. I like to think of kinship as the backbone of anthropology. Economics, politics, ritual, subsistence, and every other major theme within anthropology operate within contexts that intersect with kinship. The extent to which kinship is rhetorically prominent varies considerably across cultures, but it's always somewhere in the mix. In Pakistan, it is easier to identify and study because it figures so prominently in how Pakistanis talk about their own societies and identities.

A South Asian Diaspora friend of mine once described her South Asian father as a master of emotional blackmail. Her parents wanted her to marry a suitable young man. She had been in a stable relationship at university for several years and her parents had known and partially approved of it. But when she graduated, it was time for her to get serious and marry an appropriate person. That means someone of the same caste and sect with comparable income and educational levels. Up until that point, I assumed that she was as individually oriented as any British or American undergraduate student. She came in to the university one day and told me that she'd broken up with her longstanding boyfriend and was in the process of reviewing eligible young men proposed by her mother and aunties. I was shocked and asked how on earth her parents managed to persuade her to take this decision. She said her father had started packing all of his belongings into a small room in the back of the house and said he was going to move in there and never show his face in the community again. The shame of his daughter marrying outside the faith was too much to bear. She told me there was a lot of crying and yelling, but in the end, she realized that she loved her family, despite being cross with them, and she couldn't do something that she knew would hurt them so profoundly. I have often pondered why her parents, who were well established in the UK, were so traumatized by the prospect of their daughter marrying a non-Muslim, non-South Asian origin man. I have concluded that while South Asians are diverse and there are undoubtedly many exceptions to this generalization, are socialized to prioritize their families in ways that are difficult for British and North Americans to fully grasp. With time, I have also come to suspect that it is, in fact, what we might loosely label Anglo-Saxon origin societies that are the deviant ones globally. It seems that rather than ask why Pakistanis and other South Asian groups are *so* focused on their families, it would make better sense to ask why British and North Americans are relatively less interested in, and certainly less compliant with, their families.

If kinship is the backbone upon which human societies are built, and through which so much human communication happens, then it stands to reason that all anthropologists must spend some time understanding how the kinship system of their chosen group operates. It is not equally rhetorically significant in all societies, but it's important everywhere. In order to study kinship, we need to look at the *actions* of kinship. What does it do? We can ask people what it means, and that matters and is worth doing, but this isn't just an esoteric domain of ritual meaning making. Kinship has tangible consequences in society that can be observed and measured. There are two obvious domains that fall under the kinship umbrella: alliance and descent. Each of these has transactional expressions that fortunately are typically very public in Pakistan. Actual childbirth is certainly not open for public spectators, but the birth of a child is not normally a secret in Pakistan—indeed it is a cause for celebration that is both public and usually uncontroversial (potential questions of dubious paternity aside).

DESCENT

Descent is one of the most common idioms for self-identification in Pakistan. The National Database & Registration Authority (NADRA) in Pakistan *requires* descent information to identify individuals before they will issue identity cards or passports. When I first turned up in my little Punjabi village in early 1998, everyone I met introduced themselves and others to me with a name and a *qaum* identifier. If I had already met one of the person's relatives, I was typically given a brief pedigree summary to tell me how they were connected. When there was no actual genealogical connection, sometimes one was "invented" in a fuzzy way that I only learned later was meant to indicate affection rather than actual lineage. The affection was real, but I came to learn later that it was never mistaken for "real" kinship. The emphasis on *biradari* was striking. It mattered to local people in a way that I hadn't grasped when I had lived in Pakistan as a teenager. On one occasion, I told my village friends that I had gone to a school with a prominent Pakistani politician. They got very excited and told me he was a Gujar, like them. I hadn't known that, or if I had, it hadn't made much of an impression. A few weeks later, I happened to speak to the friend on the phone and, feeling rather smugly proud of myself, I said to him, "I gather you're a Gujar, like my friends here." He said that of course he was a Gujar and was shocked that I hadn't known that. He wasn't really angry, but he did that *faux* injured thing of pretending that I had been a terrible friend for not being aware of something so fundamental about him. I honestly don't know how I managed to live in Pakistan through half of my high school without picking up on the importance of *qaum*—or to be honest, without even picking up on the *existence* of *qaum*. I assumed that since I hadn't noticed it, it must not have been important to my urban Lahori friends. Only many years later did I appreciate that they all knew who was who and it was only because I didn't know enough to even ask the right questions that they didn't think to teach me overtly some things that were ubiquitous to them.

NASL AND PATRILINEALITY

I first encountered local representations of human conception in rural Punjab in the late 1990s. I was talking to a relative of my host and he asked me how I thought babies were made. I said that the father and mother each provided a gamete and these were combined inside the woman. The resulting embryo then attached itself to the wall of the mother's uterus where it received all the nutrients it needed to develop into a fetus and ultimately a baby. He was clearly dissatisfied with this answer and explained to me that the mother really had no role in providing what he called the germ, using the English word. He was sure that it was the man's germ alone which was implanted in the woman's uterus. The woman did indeed provide nutrients, but she transmitted none of her own substance. In addition, my description of conception left out the breath of Allah. This happens along with the physical development of the fetus and it is this miraculous, divine intervention, which transforms the cells from being lifeless organic matter into a living, soul bearing being which will become a human.

Chapter 4

The Qur'an devotes several Surat to parenthood, some of which hint at varying models of conception. Khalifa's (1989) translation of Sura 23 al-Mu'minun (The Believers), verses 12–14, in particular says:

[23:12] We created the human being from a certain kind of mud.

[23:13] Subsequently we reproduced him from a tiny drop, that is placed into a well-protected repository.

[23:14] Then we developed the drop into a hanging (embryo), then developed the hanging (embryo) into a bite sized (fetus), then created the bite sized (fetus) into bones, then covered the bones with flesh. We thus produce a new creature. Most blessed is GOD, the best creator. (al-Mu'minum 23: 12–14)[2]

Some version of this Sura is invoked as evidence that the production of children is a consequence of a man's seminal fluid combined with the blessing of God. Women are relegated to the status of "well protected repository" or safe lodging. The emphasis on women as repositories or lodgings reinforces traditional patrilineal descent group organization and inheritance and justifies both the exclusion of women from land inheritance and the importance of controlling women's sexuality. If there were a possibility that a woman might have had sex with an unauthorized man, then it may result in a man unknowingly socially fathering someone else's child who might not share the essential essence of the man or his lineage. The child would potentially have no "real" relatives in the house in which he or she is being brought up.

On one occasion, when speaking in English to Sardar Jehangir, a young man in northern Punjab, he told me that his mother was not part of his family. I was surprised and asked how that was possible. When he switched to Urdu, the sentence made more sense. She was not part of his *biradari*, but she was his *rishta*. *Rishta* is the more inclusive notion of related people and includes people related by marriage. *Biradari*, on the other hand, is a more restrictive concept based on patrilineal descent.[3] Given the prevalence of close cousin marriage, it is very common for mothers to come from the same *biradari*. It was therefore notable that the young man I was speaking to had a mother who did *not* come from his *biradari*.

Since the creation of children is a result of a man's sperm, God's will and a women's "protected repository" it is therefore unsurprising that a person's *nasl*, or "breed," is derived solely from his or her father. Choudry Mustafa,[4] a rural landowner in northern Punjab, explained to me that there is a fundamental problem with portraying Bilawal Zardari, the son of Benazir Bhutto as a Bhutto. He is a Zardari, I was told, because his *nasl* can *only* come from his father, Asif Ali Zardari. His mother, Choudry Mustafa told me, was indeed a Bhutto, but she was not capable of transmitting the essence of Bhutto-ness to her children. The *real* inheritor of Zulfikar Ali Bhutto, Choudry Mustafa argued, were the children of Benazir Bhutto's deceased brother. He was also critical of the Muslim League's attempts to promote Nawaz Sharif's daughter, Mariam Nawaz, as the inheritor of her father's political essence. He accepted that she shares his *nasl*, but said that she cannot pass it on to her children and therefore was not an appropriate political leader.

The argument is akin to a model of leadership and inheritance that maps neatly onto other social institutions. Sufi *khilafat*, for example, are a type of intellectual franchise in which a master authorizes his pupils to open their own religious centers modeled on the original institution[5]. Such *khilafat* are authenticated through a process very close to recounting genealogical origins. Most important shrines in Punjab, derive their authenticity not directly from events or people associated with the specific area, but from older institutions and lineages. One of the most famous *silsila*, spiritual lineages, in South Asia, is the Chishti order. Chishti saints trace their spiritual lineage from the cousin of the Prophet Mohammad, 'Alī ibn Abī Ṭālib. This provides a type of certification that Chishti saints are doubly *bona fide* because they have both the physical descent connection, or *nasl*, as well as the spiritual and intellectual transmission from their forefathers.

The transmission of sufi authenticity is derived both from the physical transmission, what my friend Choudry Mustafa calls *nasl*, as well as the nurture and education provided by religious teachers. Both are required for the production and maintenance of a "real" *khilafat*. Similarly, the reproduction of a *biradari* requires that the male contribution to the production of children is known with confidence plus the right nurturing environment in which the specialist household knowledge will be provided. Such specialist knowledge may seem trivial to outsiders, but it signals membership in the correct group. Women are instrumental in providing the post-partum environment in which children learn the specialist household knowledge. This may include the right type of *chapatti* or flat bread which is to be considered delicious, or a specific set of lullabies to sing to children. Other families may share much of the ostensibly specialist knowledge, and that may make marriage between such groups more or less challenging.

This idealized model of procreation means that land inheritance, one of the most important material expressions of a household, has not historically included women. When I first lived in a landlord dominated village in Attock District in 1998, I was told that women should not inherit land because it would mean that ultimately the land would be inherited by children from a different *biradari*. In other words, land would leave the "family," in the sense that Sardar Jehangir meant when he said that his mother was not part of his family.

Chapter 4

THE THREAT OF MATERNAL TRANSMISSION

For a few years after I concluded my initial doctoral research in northern Punjab, I thought I understood what local people believed about conception and essence transmission within families, but then, in 2007, one of my landlord friends in northern Punjab had a small role in a Punjabi television drama called *Janu Malukan*. A television production company had identified his village as a suitable location in which to film a drama set in rural Punjab. In order to entice the landlord into allowing them to use his land and village for their film, they offered to let him play a Punjabi landlord in the film. He had one scene in which he played a version of himself. I watched this drama and was impressed not only at my friend's acting ability, but also the power of the story. It is a moral tale about the evils of young people choosing their own marriage partner. I watched this film in the company of other landlords and non-landowning village men. I took my laptop to the village tea shop and watched the film with different groups of men and asked them what they thought the moral of the drama might be.

The drama begins in the home of a wealthy landlord. Khan Sahib (played by the famous actor Jameel Fakhri) is reclining on a *charpai*, a traditional South Asian cot, surrounded by servants. A young man named Janu is massaging the landlord's legs while another peasant plays an instrument. He sends the poor young man inside his house to take his hookah away. Inside, we discover that the young man and the daughter of the landlord have a close relationship. In fact, they are in love. Through the course of seeing them meet secretly under the village banyan tree, we learn that the daughter wants to be with Janu, but she is afraid that her father may try to arrange a marriage for her with someone else. Janu tells her that they can run away together and live happily, if her father tries to arrange a marriage with someone else. Shortly after, Khan Sahib is riding on horseback while falcon hunting through the mountains. Janu and other peasants are around him on foot managing the hunting dog and the falcon. Janu tells Khan Sahib that they can go home because they have already caught four *theether* (pheasants) and that must be enough for everyone. Khan Sahib says that they must get more because Merbahn Khan, another big landowner, is coming to the house. He is arranging a marriage between Merbahn Khan's son and his own daughter. Khan Sahib and the other peasants continue on, but Janu is stunned and freezes in place. His friend, a fellow peasant, holds him and asks him what is wrong. Janu is held by his friend while he visibly seems to collapse as his romantic dreams crumble before him. Janu and the girl arrange to run away together. His friend provides Janu with a mare to take them both far away. Late at night, the girl sneaks out of her father's home to meet Janu. Janu, meanwhile, is thanking his friend for the gift of a mare and is about to leave the animal stables to go meet his beloved. As he is leaving, his friend stops him and says that he must avoid water with the mare. He says that the mare's mother was afraid of water and would run away when near rivers. Janu hears the advice and then abruptly freezes. He looks stricken and his friend, again, wants to know what is wrong. Janu sits down and says that he cannot leave with his love. His friend asks why and he explains that if he leaves with his love and they then have a daughter, then his daughter may run away from him when she grows up. The drama then fades to the present day when Janu is an old man sitting under the same banyan tree where he plotted his romantic future with his former lover. His wife, daughter, and granddaughter all come to get him to come back to the house. We see that while he still pines for his soul mate, he is happy because he had a good daughter who married who she was supposed to and he has a granddaughter who will, like her mother and grandmother, obey her father's wishes.

The drama represents an old trope in South Asian cinema and television. Young people may rebel against parental control but ultimately, everyone's happiness is more likely if they accept such guidance and do what parents, especially mothers, want them to do. Parental love and control is a common motif in South Asian cinema and television. In the political film about communal riots, *Zakhm,* for example, a man abandons his wife and their two small children when his mother douses herself in kerosene and tries to light a match to immolate herself. Her devoted son falls to his knees and begs his mother to forgive him and promises he will leave his wife and will marry a good Hindu woman of his mother's choosing. The film takes place across different times as it shows the tragic outcome for the abandoned wife and children. The message is clear, love marriages, or perhaps more accurately unauthorized love more generally, result in pain and suffering for everyone.

Janu Malukan provides an interesting Punjabi twist to the admonition against love marriage however. It is not just that love marriages cause distress and misery for everyone involved, they also increase the likelihood that the female offspring of the unions will disobey their parents. Janu presumably believes that he is able to provide an appropriate environment in which his daughters can develop and grow. He must believe that he is capable to bringing up a daughter who will be well behaved and obedient, but he loses confidence in his ability to do so with a woman who was willing to disobey her own father. That suggests that there may be some kind of character transmission from mother to daughter. While such a notion is hardly challenging in societies which trace their descent through both matrilineal and patrilineal directions, it presents a contradiction of both the principle of agnatic lineality and Qur'anic descriptions of how children are created.

Chapter 4

PUNJABI TRANSMISSION OF PERSONHOOD

Personhood is constituted from a combination of social interactions, positioning within social networks and ideas of descent. Marriott's (1976) seminal description of dividuality, or partible personhood, describes an important concept in how individuals are understood. Among Hindu groups, such a notion helps to explain the extremes of caste segregation. While Pakistani Muslims reject the idea of ritual purity and pollution which might justify the discrimination experienced by Untouchable Hindus in India, they nevertheless are concerned with dirt and contagion. The justification for avoiding direct contact with some people is grounded in the vocabulary of filth and dirt (*gandey logon*—dirty people), but it does not extend to refusing to let such people eat from the same food containers or sit in the same seats of the buses. People seen to be "dirty" are expected to eat and drink *after* "clean" or *sharif* (noble) people, but they may use the same dishes. Muslims do not typically refuse to shake hands with anyone, but they only offer their fingertips to low-caste, "dirty" people. When hugging, they may hold their hand out and stop the other person's chest from coming into direct contact with their own. In other words, Pakistani Muslims are apparently as subject to Marriott's notion of dividuality, as opposed to *in*dividuality.

It may be that Janu's problem is that a mother might contaminate her daughter through contact. If so, then the process must be extremely subtle since Janu would also be influencing his daughter's upbringing and could, and presumably would, put a halt to any subversive socialization which appeared to be encouraging his daughter to choose her own path in life. If it were only this Punjabi drama that we had to go by, then not only would this be a real possibility, it would also probably not be a terribly interesting story to analyze. However, early on in my public viewings of *Janu Malukan*, a curious thing began to happen. Men started to laughingly tell me that they had been told this story by old women in their families. No one said that they heard the story from their parents. The story seems to be transmitted mostly from old aunts (normally referred to as *massi*, mother's sister, or *poupi*, father's sister) or sometimes grandmothers (*dadi*, father's mother or *nani*, mother's mother). The story sounds slightly more cryptic than the Pakistan Television drama, which may have made it not only more memorable, but perhaps also more implicitly powerful.

Young men are cautioned not to try and run away with a girl because there was a mare who was afraid of water and whose female offspring were also afraid of water. The *massi* did not, apparently elaborate and make it explicit that the daughter of a *human* woman who ran away from her father would *also* run away from her own father (in other words, the man who had "stolen" her mother). Young men understood the point of the story without such elaboration because it is a message that gets reinforced in a number of different ways in rural Punjab.

The folk warning about mares being used as a moral lesson about human women, introduces the problem, however, that the problem may be insurmountable regardless of the nurturing environment in which the daughter grows up. So even if a young man is convinced that he is in love and the love of his life is going to be an ideal mother, *massi's* message is clear—something of the character of the mother *will* get passed on to the daughter. In other words, a woman's person is partially shaped by some direct substance transmission from her *mother*. She will certainly be seen as *belonging* to her father's *nasl*, but tales like this suggest rather strongly that traditional Punjabi notions of the construction of persons do not casually or easily dismiss women's essential contribution to children.

There is considerable evidence that gender requires active socialization and training. Marsden's (2007) account of the production of masculinity in Chitral suggests that while one's *nasl* may come from the father, that is insufficient for establishing satisfactory masculinity or manliness. That involves a sustained apprenticeship in the appropriate values. Women too must learn how to be appropriately feminine both in Punjabi and Pukhtun communities (Eglar 1960; Grima 1992).

The idea that mothers transmit some aspects of personality and character is therefore compatible with local notions of both personal contagion and the mechanisms by which important social attributes are acquired. This is curious, however, given the rhetorical insistence that children are the product of patrilineal substance, Allah's breath and the protective repository of a mother's womb.

KINSHIP TERMINOLOGIES

In the first chapter of this book, I mentioned the study of the formal classificatory aspects of kinship as well as the messier practices associated with kin groups and relations. This is nowhere more evident than in ethnographic research, where kinship terminology is unquestionably worth learning, regardless of where one does fieldwork. Learning kin terminologies can be tedious and it takes patience to determine the boundaries of kinship terminologies, especially when adopting a systematic approach, like Leaf's kin elicitation method (1972). Anthropologists have devised a number of methods for generating kin terms and they all have their merits. Some anthropologists haven't worried much about whether they've got complete terminologies, because their interest has been mapping genealogies or pedigrees rather than developing a comprehensive understanding of the linguistic logic of kin terms. The classic anthropological method for generating genealogical data, Rivers genealogical method, was one of the early techniques to emerge from actually going out in the field. W.H.R. Rivers was not a participant observer, like the generation that came after, but he did participate in serious fieldwork. He adopted what we would now describe as a rather ethnocentric approach to eliciting genealogies, assuming that the basic kin terms that are relevant in English must be similar to those in other languages. During the Torres Straits expedition (from which *a lot* of really interesting anthropological ideas have sprung), he identified 6 key kin terms: father, mother, brother, sister, son, daughter (Rivers 1900). From those, he produced his genealogies and they were very handy and provided a great deal of data for certain kinds of analysis. Sadly, they were also imposing a particular set of constraints on the genealogies that risked misrepresenting critical differences between the kinship terminologies. Kin terms are one way of organizing relationships in groups. They reflect aspects of who matters to whom and how. In English, affinal, or in-law kin, get an extension of the consanguineal terms. So my "brother" is a person with whom I share at least one parent. My "brother-in-law" is someone with whom I share a marriage connection either through my sister, my spouse, or in an increasing number of countries around the world, my brother. English does not provide me with what I would call an irreducible, or "basic" kin term, akin to Berlin and Kay's basic color terms (1999) of relations by marriage, apart from my spouse (husband or wife). The offspring of the affinal relation, in contrast, *do* generate basic kin terms (uncle, aunt, nephew, niece, cousin), so there are *some* affinal relations that generate basic kin terms even in the absence of any shared consanguinity. The offspring of my spouse's siblings are *my* nieces and nephews, despite sharing no known descent relations.

In Urdu, on the other hand, both consanguineal kin (shared descent) and some affinal kin (marriage) get unique kin terms. A man's sister's husband is his *salaa*. His brother's wife is his *bhobi*. Each of these basic terms comes with a set of reciprocal expectations about behavior and can be understood as normative representations of how people are connected to one another. The complete set of affinal kin terms is not as extensive as the complete set of descent terms, but it's enough to substantially increase one's kin network. In practice, people may choose consanguineous terms rather than affinal terms when addressing one another. In particular, sons-in-law (*damadh*) would be unlikely to address their mothers-in-law as *saas*, but would typically adopt whatever term of address their wife uses with her parents. Like the descent kin terms, gender and relative age are built into some of the terms, reflecting the importance of age hierarchy within households.

Another distinction between English and Urdu is the bifurcation by sex of parent. In English, kin terms of paternal and maternal sides mirror one another exactly, at least in formal standard English. In practice, there can be idiosyncratic conventions that allow people to distinguish paternal from maternal grandparents. One of the possibly statistically significant trends I have come across in the many years I've been teaching British students is a possible distinction between maternal and paternal grandparents, especially grandmothers among working-class English people. It's not a "rule" but over the years, I counted more maternal grandmothers referred to as "Nan," while paternal grandmothers were called "Gran." The trend seems to be entirely unconscious and so falls short of having any prescriptive power, but the fact that over the years, students who identify as working class are more likely to use the Nan/Gran distinction than not is one of those interesting tidbits that will have to be left to someone else to investigate properly. Urdu, and most other South Asian languages make a critical distinction between paternal and maternal kin. Both are important and they appear to be equally elaborate, though see Leaf (1972) for a possible extra paternal elaboration among Punjabi Sikhs. Leaf's thoroughly generated kin term map for Punjab Sikhs would suggest that patrilineal grandparents extend one generation deeper than matrilineal grandparents. Apparently for Punjabi Sikhs it is possible to use the term *pardada* (great grandfather- paternal), but not *parnana* (great grandfather-maternal). The people with whom he worked agreed that one could not say *parnana*. In northern Punjab, I found Punjabi Muslims far less strict about the notion, though I admit that I have never heard them use the term *parnana* except to confirm to me that such a term was possible. This too is perhaps a question that can no longer be answered satisfactorily because their use of kin terms is now strongly affected by their knowledge of English kin terms and their exposure to different languages via broadcast and internet media.

The reason I am taking the trouble to explain some of the basics of Urdu kin terminology is because it reflects differences in between the linguistic structure of Urdu and English kinship, family, lineage, household, and caste. Urdu terms provide significantly more precision about *how* people are related in relation to one another. Read (2001), through the course of a substantial corpus of research on kinship terminologies and specifically kinship algebras, has demonstrated the extent to which all kin terms can be derived from a pretty narrow subset of kin terms. And that in practice, any native speaker of a language, will be able to derive the correct kin term from knowing the kin terms of two other people. Ego (the native speaker) must know what kin terms are used between themselves and Person A and what kin terms are used between Person A and Person B, in order to know what kin terms should be used between Ego and Person B. I say terms, because except in a very few cases, kin terms are reciprocal but different (the exceptions being sibling terms—in English, same sex siblings use the same reciprocal term for one another). This means, that if I refer to Person A as mother, and Person A refers to Person B as sister, then I know I should call person B, aunt or auntie (in English). The same is roughly true for other kin terms, though there are kin terms where native speakers might need to know additional knowledge, such as the sex of Ego. In traditional Kakabila kin terminology, for example, the relative sex of the speaker and reference was a critical determinant, rather than the sex of the person being spoken to. For example, in English, I use the term sister because *she's* female, but in Kakabila Miskitu, siblings of the *same* sex refer to one another with one term, while siblings of opposite sex use another (Jamieson 1998). Such systems are not at all unusual around the world, though they are a bit surprising for native English speakers.

PERSONHOOD, SUBSTANCE AND LANGUAGE

I have tried to show in this chapter that fundamental ideas of personhood and substance transmission are integral to ideas of kinship. This affects not only the concept of kinship, but also has implications for the constraints how kinship can function and what can be done with kinship. The linguistic structure of kinship terminologies imposes ideas about relations that have concrete impacts on how individuals relate to one another. To be sure, there are pragmatic decisions that people can and do make that draw on other idea systems to deal with opportunities and obstacles, but these aren't pure invention, rather they should be understood as creative re-purposing of available ideas. As with other forms of reproduction, such re-purposing can result in adaptive mutations of core ideas of personhood over time, but one of the abiding questions in cultural anthropology is not why cultural concepts are so flexible, but instead, why they aren't *more* flexible given how easily humans can contradict and manipulate them to suit particular contingencies (see especially Sperber 1985). The fact that cultural concepts persist, despite being manipulated and twisted to address *ad hoc* demands speaks volumes about the economy of knowledge production and the utility of replicable idea systems that are subject to communicative constraints.

Among rural landowners, there is considerable benefit to a heavily patrilineal concept of procreation that can serve to justify particular forms of resource transmission and control. There are more facets of everyday life than *just* land ownership and transmission, however, so the strong emphasis on patrilineal procreation is not universally fit for all contexts. The ability to retain a politically powerful idea while nevertheless acting in contradiction to that idea, is not only pragmatically useful, I argue it is crucial for survival. Personhood is tied to relationality in any community and the conferment of particular categories of person trigger rights to resources, decision making, and prestige. When the primary category would result in a loss of resource, an inability to control key decisions, or a reduction in prestige, there can be two responses. A population could either revolutionize the idea system underpinning the practices and risk losing an important political justification for the future, *or* draw on alternative idea systems without creating an overly constraining precedent that would undo an important tool for maintaining the status quo.

NOTES

1. Nor, however, am I asserting that kinship was *not* the first social institution. I make no claims about the chronological order of social institutions.

2. To be fair, not all translations are quite so skewed toward unique patrilineal substance transmission. Regardless of the translation or interpretation in scholarly circles, however, there is a clear and repeated rhetoric of the importance of patrilineal substance.

3. *Biradari* is also used as a synonym for *zat* or caste in some cases, though *zat* was not a common term in the village in which I worked. *Zat* is an endogamous descent group.

4. All names are pseudonyms.

5. But see Werbner (2003) for an account of the role of charisma and personality in the creation of religious devotion in relation to a particular Nakshbandi sufi saint.

Chapter 5

Kinship and Conflict Management at the Local Level

INTRODUCTION

In this chapter, I look at the role of kin groups in managing conflict at local levels. While the villages in which I have worked are not renowned for endemic blood feud, they do have notably persistent land disputes that occasionally become extremely tense. Conflict is part of all human societies and the tools for managing conflict have formed an important domain of analysis within anthropology. At least as far back as Maine (1861), anthropologists have recognized that careful examination of how societies deal with serious conflict reveals a great deal about other aspects of cultural and social values, norms, and behaviors. When one of Hoebel's Cheyenne informants asked him why he spent so much time focusing on the conflicts, when there was a lot more going on that people arguing, he replied that it was when people transgressed that he could identify the boundaries of the culture (Llewellyn and Hoebel 1941). Local conflicts in rural Pakistan are inseparable from kinship. Not only do conflicts frequently occur within kin groups, but they rely on kin for their management and ultimate resolution. Equally importantly, kinship itself is often the trigger for conflict. The very structures that create and maintain relations between people lay the seeds for competition and conflict. The first part of the chapter provides a brief summary of the literature on conflict and its management in Pakistan and north India. The emphasis of multiple ethnographers and the people they worked with on maintaining and managing disputes reveals a great deal about the importance of kinship categories and relations. I use one particularly turbulent period of local land disputes in a rural part of northern Punjab, in which the key participants were effectively at "war" in their own village for almost four years. This land dispute is telling because it pitted close cousins against one another and fundamentally re-drew the earlier factional boundaries that I had witnessed in the village in the decade leading up to the dispute. I was able to observe, close up, the collapse of some well-established factions and the painful process of reforming those factions over the four-year period. By this point in my relationship with the landlords in this village, I was able to speak directly to older women in the village and learned a great deal more about their involvement in land conflicts. In other parts of Pakistan, kinship is intimately involved in conflict, both in triggering escalation as well as in defusing and preventing violent outbursts. By focusing on ethnographic cases, it is possible to identify the role of kinship ideologies in driving some of the justifications used for faction building, but it is clear that kinship alone is insufficient to explain the alliances that emerge.

Throughout my time working with Punjabi landlords, I have found myself in awe at their audacity, ingenuity, and resilience. I can think of few areas in which I have been more impressed than their ability to handle serious conflict. The men with whom I have worked can push their disputes right to the edge of violence and beyond. They are able to live under the constant pressure of knowing that they may be the intended target of acts of violent brutality while never losing their ability to live life. They continue to enjoy socializing and joking with friends and family. They don't put their lives on hold while they "deal" with conflict, but instead, forge ahead with every task, however routine or trivial. They struggle hard to win their disputes, but even when they "lose," they pick themselves up and keep chipping away to ensure the survival of themselves and their households. Perhaps the thing that I most admire about the landlords I have known in north and central Punjab, is their near infinite capacity to put aside animosities when they no longer serve any purpose. So rather than holding a grudge forever, they hold a grudge only so long as it makes sense. They can restore friendly relations with almost all enemies if that is what serves their household's interests most effectively. The longer I watch these landlords in action, the more convinced I become that this has been an essential survival strategy. It is clearly possible to sustain near constant animosity within a community, and I cite several ethnographic examples in this chapter in which that appears to be the case, but there are particular circumstances in which those societies are able to maintain the chronic states of feuding tensions.

DISPUTE IN PAKISTAN

The ethnography of Pakistan has a long tradition of focusing on the ways in which local communities manage conflict. This is perhaps partly the result of the ways that these communities were framed by the colonial descriptions of certain groups as "martial" or "warlike." Colonial era Gazetteers casually described particular caste groups with sweeping characterizations that linger today in subtle and not so subtle forms.[1] In the ethnographic accounts of Pakistan produced from independence through to the early 2000s, I suggested that there existed an invisible dividing line that cut through Pakistan that owes as much to the *a priori* literature upon which research designs were based as it does to the empirical observations from the field (Lyon 2004). The so-called tribal areas fit more closely with the literature generated from Middle Eastern ethnography, while the so called peasant areas belonged firmly within an Indian subcontinental ethnographic tradition. I suggested that at least part of the cause of this distinction could be attributed to the literature the anthropologists read prior to going to the field. The area in which I carried out my first extended fieldwork happened to fall geographically between the big divide of tribal and peasant. Consequently, I read extensively from both traditions (South Asian and Middle Eastern) and, perhaps predictably, encountered substantial evidence of *both* tribalism and peasantry in the field.

The ethnography of conflict in Pakistan and northern India over the past 70 years suggests that there are some commonly found patterns for managing conflict, but they are not necessarily effective or possible in all circumstances. There are areas of Pakistan that are only loosely under the direct authority of the Pakistan state or its constituent provinces. The most famous of these is the former Federally Administered Tribal Areas (FATA), and the Provincially Administered Tribal Areas (PATA). Barth's seminal work in the Swat Valleys provided ample ethnographic evidence of the ways in which chronic rivalry and potential conflict can be managed sustainably (Barth 1959a, 1959b, 1981). The constant jockeying for advantage among the landowning Khans in Swat, Barth says, could, and did, erupt into violence, but it was not entirely uncontrollable and there were clear pathways to defusing open conflict and preventing actual bloodshed. Lindholm (1982), a generation later, describes a world in which *tarburwali*, cousin rivalry or enmity (more on this later) touched every facet of life in the Pukhtun communities in which he and his wife, Cherry, carried out fieldwork in the 1970s. Keiser's (1991) analysis of a feuding area of Kohistan in northwest Pakistan, near the Afghan border, makes clear that while the violence is real, it is culturally meaningful and socially regulated. He argues that an overly simplified application of Darwinian natural selection neglects the sociocultural relations inherent in institutions such as blood feud. Like Black-Michaud (1975), Keiser sees a functional aspect of blood feud as constructing transactional social relations, arguably understood as a form of negative Maussian gift (1966).

Carrying out fieldwork in areas marked by rhetoric that valorizes and glorifies feud and conflict can be challenging. The severity and longevity of conflicts in some parts of traditional Pakistan pose genuine risks to visitors.

In what might be described as a real life, modern day *boy's own adventure,* Frembgen (2014), recounts pretty harrowing tales of open gun battles and, on one occasion, a hasty retreat from fieldwork during a feud between rival cousins in the Harban Valley of Kohistan. The village was entirely oriented around such feuds. Families constructed well defended watch towers and social relations were fraught with mistrust. Frembgen spent almost a decade returning to the village to earn the trust of his hosts and their neighbors. He described a climate of suspicion and what can only be described as heightened paranoia about the ill-intentions of others. But even in this environment of persistent and seemingly all-encompassing conflict, Frembgen found a routine of life that adjusted around the disruption. What distinguishes areas like this from the parts of Punjab in which I have worked, is partly the greater presence and control of the state, but also notably more intricate cross cutting marital networks linking households.

CONFLICT MEDIATION INSTITUTIONS

In India and Pakistan, there are two well-known customary institutions charged with managing, or even resolving, conflict: *jirga* in the northern parts of Pakistan, and *panchayat* in the plains of northern India (see Chaudhary 1999 for a concise description of the legal pluralism found in north India and Pakistan). These are not poles apart, but their composition and authority can vary in different places. In my experience of listening to stories about *jirga* in northern Punjab over two decades, it has become clear that there is little constraint on how, when or why *jirga* might be formed. The truism that all conflict happens about women, gold or land (*zan, zar, zamin*) is certainly not strictly, true, but probably does account for all the cases dealt with by *jirga*. *Jirga* are somewhere between mediation and arbitration. They have some authority to impose decisions, though this is not strictly vested in the *jirga per se,* but rather with the power and position of the members of the *jirga*. *Panchayat*, similarly, also appear to rely on the authority of the membership, rather than the powers inherent to the council of respected caste leaders.

Conflict mediation/arbitration councils, like courts in Britain or the United States, are embedded with the cultures and societies in which they exist. Madsen's (1991) careful analysis of *panchayat* in the north Indian state of Uttar Pradesh, demonstrates the seemingly impossible challenge faced by *panchayat*. Madsen's example is useful because he worked in a Hindu area of north India, where notions of *varna* are relevant. In the Muslim area of Punjab in which I have worked, there is virtually no talk of *varna*. When asked, local people in the area take educated guesses about which *varna* their *qaum* might be, but they aren't entirely certain and do not always agree among themselves. So it is interesting to note the contrasts as well as the continuities between a Hindu Indian and a Muslim Pakistani peasant village. In the villages that Madsen studied in the early 1980s, the common pattern was for a single caste to dominate the arable land. The farmers were not large landowners and worked the land with their own household members. The exception were Rajput and Brahmin dominated villages, in which they tended to be minorities within their village and reliant on sharecroppers from other "lower" castes. The latter is a better comparison with the common pattern in the rainfed areas of Attock District, perhaps because of the insecurity of rainfed agriculture.[2] In any event, the concept of caste equality is of considerable importance to the local farmers. This adherence to equality exists alongside the unmistakable hierarchy between castes, and especially between *varna*. The case that Madsen discusses to illustrate the tensions of equality and hierarchy deals with villages dominated by members of the Jat caste. One of the principle responsibilities of caste *panchayat* in Uttar Pradesh, according to Madsen, is the regulation of marriage to ensure the critical principle of equality between clans or *gotra* is retained. Marriage is considered to involve ranked relations between the families, because fundamentally, there is an asymmetry between wife-takers and wife-givers. No marriage should, however, result in any compromise to the principle of equality between the *gotra*. The *panchayat* are therefore charged with carefully assessing the genealogies of marriage partners to ensure that all Jat *gotra* remain equal. Madsen argues that *panchayat* are incapable of really reconciling the tensions of ranked marriage and equal *gotra*. They are more successful in mobilizing all clans against a common external enemy, but less so in a domestic domain that can trigger serious conflict.

Customary conflict management councils across north India and Pakistan exhibit common patterns. They are not bound by precedent, like either state or *shari'a* courts. The appointment of council membership is done with the knowledge and consent of the litigants. The councils can hear any evidence they choose and decide on a case by case basis, which evidence will bear on their decisions. In practice, they can hear evidence from people who, by their own admission, know nothing about the specific case being litigated, but know something about the back story that may or may not be relevant. Sometimes, witnesses may not even know much of the back story, but they would be impacted by decisions handed down from the councils and so they may be asked or allowed to comment before the councils. Finally, one of the recurring aspects of *jirga* that I have witnessed in northern Punjab, is that their power to force all litigants to accept decisions varies a great deal. *Jirga* do not have the power of the state. Sometimes, litigants reject *jirga* decisions and proceed to using state courts and filing First Information Report (FIR) with the police against one another. Occasionally, they resort to violence during or after a *jirga* hearing to try and eliminate their enemy, though this comes with considerable risk, so remains relatively uncommon. They are most effective in areas in which the state is least present. This is to be expected, of course, because when the consequences of loss are high, litigants will exhaust every vehicle to try and advance their own position. When the stakes are *zan, zar,* or *zamin,* then the potential losses are very high indeed.

COUSIN RIVALRY

Ethnographic studies of Pukhtun communities have identified a particular emphasis on cousin rivalry which is sometimes better characterized as cousin *enmity*. The word for cousin, *tarbur,* is loaded with conflicting emotional nuances. On the one hand, one's *tarbur* is potentially one's closest ally in conflict (Ahmed 1980; Barth 1959a; Lindholm 1982). Patrilateral cousins share obligations of mutual support and have a common stake in protecting the reputation of the lineage group. If there are challenges to the honor of the group, then patrilateral cousins are a reliable source of support in resolving the problems. On the other hand, they share a common ancestor from whom inherited wealth may have come. They may therefore have some legitimate claim to that wealth. Given the often confused and uncertain circumstances of postmortem resource transmission, it is no wonder that people's versions of how land or other wealth was distributed can vary. So the word for agnatic cousin, *tarbur,* is simultaneously the root word for cousin rivalry/enmity, *taburwali.*

In non-literate communities, where the record of asset distribution may rely heavily on a small number of external specialists, each cousin may have learned a slightly different version of how the allocations were agreed. One thing that has come across in almost every significant land dispute I have witnessed over the years is that all land is not equal, so even if all inheritors received the same number of square meters of land, that doesn't necessarily mean they will all feel like they're received a "just" share of the inheritance. So *tarbur*, or agnatic cousins, may not be the most suitable allies in all conflict.

In Punjab, the phenomenon of cousin rivalry/enmity is all too familiar. Punjabis also use the word for agnatic cousin, *sharik,* as the root for cousin rivalry/enmity, *sharika.* When I first encountered the term, *sharika,* I asked a friend what this meant. He laughed and said that above all, no one wanted their *sharik* to know how much money they had in the bank or how much their income was. *Sharik* are your closest relatives outside of your own immediate household which means they have a legitimate claim to your assets if they are in need. While a generous and loving individual will probably *want* to share with his or her relatives in need, only a fool would assume that in a large family everyone will be entirely honest about what constitutes a *need*. One of the many lessons I have learned at the feet of my many wise Punjabi teachers, is that it's a mistake to be too honest about one's assets. A generation before me, Fox (1969), in a careful analysis of post-independence change in rural north India, commented that the amount of land owned by an Indian farmer was directly related to how long you had known them. When he first entered the field and asked farmers how much land they owned, the total never surpassed the amount that could be held unproblematically (i.e. legally) by a single farmer. As he got to know people better, they admitted that in fact, they owned a little more than the Indian government thought a single farmer should own. By the time he left the field, he had discovered that some of the farmers owned considerably more land than they would admit to any government officials. In Pakistan, apart from brief symbolic gestures under Ayub Khan and Z. A. Bhutto in the 1960s and 1970s, Pakistani farmers have never had to worry about the government setting caps on maximum land ownership by individual farmers, so they aren't necessarily constrained by a fear of land redistribution. They are, however, constrained by expectations of mutual support in times of need within their family networks. If a farmer has boasted about his incredibly successful crop yield one year and has exaggerated his landholdings to appear more powerful and important, he may come to regret it when he is flooded with requests for aid from relatives who feel deprived. One of the privately voiced anxieties I have heard from some Pakistani Diaspora is that their relatives don't understand how expensive England is, so assume that their British resident family can provide more remittances than is actually possible. The issue has lessened with heightened awareness of the details of life outside of Pakistan, but there continue to be sporadic stories of overt hostility fueled by resentment that someone else has been given a better "deal" in life thanks to living abroad. That resentment can spill into violence on occasion. Some of the kidnappings in the Mirpur area of Kashmir are rumored to be carried out with detailed insider information. This suggests that relatives left behind may, on rare occasions, use information about income and assets to help the kidnappers set appropriate ransoms that can be paid relatively quickly through second mortgages or quick sales of assets in the UK. The moral of the stories always seem to come back to the same point—love your family, but don't share *too* much information about your wealth with them.

AN INHERITANCE DISPUTE IN NORTHERN PUNJAB

In 2011, Malik Gulzar passed away. He died surrounded by two wives, four daughters, and his unmarried sister. His only son had died in a car accident

30 years earlier and despite taking a second wife late in life, he had not produced another male heir. Malik Gulzar left a considerable portfolio of agricultural and commercial land and had been a force of stability and authority in the village for decades. Since his elder brother, Malik Muzzafar, had died a decade earlier, he had few challengers to his authority and was skilled at avoiding open confrontation with his one serious village rival—his maternal first cousin and brother-in-law. His elder brother Malik Muzaffar had four sons. The eldest and the third had emigrated decades before and spent little time in Pakistan. The second son had died a few months before Malik Gulzar. This left the youngest, Malik Liaqat, to assume the role of head of the dominant collection of households in the village. While capable as a farmer and landlord, and increasingly successful in local politics, Malik Liaqat was not universally accepted as the new leader of the village. The village was faced with a power vacuum that undermined its hard earned reputation for solidarity and stability and left it dealing with open conflict between the landowning families that persisted for almost four years. The landowners closed ranks around distinct factions and set about trying to recruit allies both in the village and beyond. They actively courted local and regional politicians offering bloc votes in elections in exchange for support in their family disputes. I had heard stories about an earlier period of open disputes in the 1970s when an earlier generation of landowner leaders had finally passed away and the next generation, the one that was firmly in control when I arrived in the late 1990s, had to jostle for position. At that time, the violence escalated to the point of Malik Muzzafar getting shot. He survived the shot, and established his reputation as a fearless and very tough landlord who was not an easy man to either dislodge or intimidate.

Between the 1970s and 2011, much had changed in Pakistan and in the village. Inheritance traditions in the village had dictated equal male inheritance of land between all surviving sons, but had excluded female heirs. Women, people said, received their inheritance premortem in the form of generous dowrys, but land was quasi sacred and had to be held in trust for future generations within the *biradari*. By 2011, however, women had benefited from higher education and they were able to develop strong arguments based on *shari'a* law that makes clear that daughters are entitled to a half share of land inheritance. It may not be equal, but it's significantly more than their mothers and grandmothers received. So when Malik Gulzar died without *any* male heir, his daughters seized the opportunity to assert their legal claims to the land. Conversations about the precise distribution of land were frequent and messy. Every time someone tried to explain the exact portion that the daughters, the widows and the sister should receive, I felt less confident that I understood *shari'a* inheritance laws at all. This was complicated further by the fact that the daughters were all married with children, so their husbands and sons sought ways to establish their claims through their female relatives. And to make things even messier, once the door to female inheritance had been opened, the other surviving sisters who had long since married out and raised their own families, remembered their own disinheritance (of land) in the 1970s and, through their sons, broached the possibility that they might claim some of the land they should have received had *shari'a* law been in force when they were young.

The disputes came to a head in 2014, when Malik Liaqat, Malik Muzaffar's youngest son, became enraged at his principle rival, Malik Iqbal, and took a gun and opened fire at Malik Iqbal's guest house (*dhera*). The other landowners of the village and surrounding villages called a massive *jirga*. The description I was given of this significant event included over 500 powerful people coming to the village and giving the leaders of the two factions an ultimatum. They had to make peace or face isolation and complete withdrawal of support. The two men had invested a great deal in developing and strengthening their factional alliances so it was difficult to let go of the energy and effort they'd invested in the rivalry. It was the father of one of the faction leaders, a lifelong rival to Malik Gulzar and his brother, who finally pleaded with his son to drop the rivalry and find a way to make peace. The details were not resolved that day, but the two men embraced and pledged to cease the open hostilities. Almost as quickly as it erupted, the disruption and chaos of a divided landowning family, subsided. Malik Liaqat and Malik Iqbal resumed socializing with one another, going to weddings together and supporting one another in land disputes with landowners from neighboring villages. Malik Iqbal pledged his voting bloc to Malik Liaqat who had been nominated to run for local office once the dispute had been resolved.

There were many disputes surrounding Malik Gulzar's inheritance. While it is possible to identify two principle factions, within them lay a number of competing interests that shifted and destabilized the delicate politics of village land conflicts. While the inclusion of women as overt litigants in the disputes may have made things appear more volatile, historical accounts of the earlier generation's jockeying for supremacy in the inheritance games would suggest that these periods of significant generational change may *always* exhibit high levels of disruption to the area.

Earlier factional boundaries could be mapped on to the geographic location of the principle Malik households in the village. The village was divided into two groups. Those who lived at the top of the small hill that formed the center of the village, were known as *Upper Walé Malik*, while those who lived at the base, were known as *Niché Walé Malik*. Both *Upper* and *Niché Walé Malik* families were descended from one of two brothers who chose not to exchange children in marriage sometime early in the nineteenth century. The reasons for their decision is unclear, but may have been linked to an argument between the brothers, or perhaps a deliberate strategy to diversify their marital networks in response to the potential threats posed by Ranjit Singh's control of Punjab. Regardless of the rationale, their decisions were repeated over the next 80–100 years and there were very few, if any, marriages between the *Upper Walé* and the *Niché Walé Malik*. This fracture in the *biradari* was brought to an end in the 1920s by two men who by all accounts were best of friends as well as being rival cousins (see Lyon 2013). The marriage between the sister of one to the other, heralded a wave of frequent marriages between *Upper* and *Niché Malik* that resulted in the geographic distinction becoming increasingly less salient with each generation. By the time I arrived in 1998, it appeared as if the geographic logic of the factions had already given way to other political factors that drove conflict alliances. The *Upper Walé* Maliks presented a coherent front both within the village and to external observers, in part because the dominant households were led by the two brothers, Malik Gulzar and his elder brother Malik Muzzaffar. Their apparent unity and the fact that they had been only two brothers to inherit all of the land from their father, meant that they had become the *de facto* leaders of the village. Among the *Niché Walé* Maliks, the picture was less coherent. The generation that might have provided the faction with appropriate leadership included more men and they clearly did not all agree on a common agenda. When I first arrived, there was a very old Malik, named Malik Mushtaq, who was said to be the 'grandfather' of the *Niché Walé Malik*, though he was clearly not literally everyone's grandfather. People estimated his age to be above 100. He died a few months after I arrived and I only had a few occasions to speak with him, but every time we met, he repeated stories about growing up with the British and the times in the 1920s and 1930s when the British District Commissioner of Campbellpur (now Attock), came to visit prominent landlords in the village. The British District Commissioner and his wife are said to have been very good friends with one of the *Upper Walé Malik* landowners and his wife. Indeed, from my very first visit to the village, I was treated to a photo show of the British district commissioner and his wife posing with smiling faces next to a very serious looking set of village landlords. Malik Mushtaq had difficulty hearing and seeing and needed some assistance to move, but when comfortably settled on his *charpai*, it was clear that his mind was intact and he remembered a great deal about the days of the British Raj. His family had done well under the British and he had been a *numberdar*[3] in the village. As a wealthy landlord who had been careful with his assets, he had managed to accumulate considerably more land in his lifetime than some of his cousins. His two sons had assumed control over their inheritance many years before my arrival in the village, so Malik Mushtaq spent his days enjoying his comfortable home and occasionally entertaining guests like me. By the time I met him, Malik Mushtaq was a kindly old man who seemed very gentle and indulgent with those around him. The tales of the determination and political clout he wielded in his younger days, however, would suggest that it would have been a grave mistake to cross him. His elder son followed in his footsteps as *numberdar* and was himself a prominent landlord who was still very active in politics and farm management when I arrived. He had begun to hand over control to his only son, Malik Iqbal. Malik Iqbal, although a relatively young man, had been given considerable freedom to manage specific aspects of the family lands and had been slowly but surely developing a reputation as a successful farmer and as a man who, like his father and grandfather, could be dangerous to cross.

Among the other *Niché Walé* Malik households, there were serious disagreements about how the elder generation's lands should have been distributed. In the late 1990s, the land disputes were ongoing despite the fact that most of the previous generation had died more than a decade before my arrival. There were a lot of male heirs among the *Niché Walé* households and while the women of these households were not, at that time, publicly involved in making claims, the general volatility and fluidity of the situation could be overwhelming at times. The disruption of the households at the base of the mountain was somewhat masked, however, because those who lived at the top of the mountain were so unified in political purpose. Whatever their internal disputes may have been, the *Upper Walé* Maliks were good at concealing them.

The process of *Upper* and *Niché* intermarriage begun 70 years before had resulted in clear bonds of loyalty that spanned the factional divide. I have written elsewhere about the proud declarations of double first cousin unions that were a regular feature of my interactions with people (Lyon 2004). As I collected genealogies of the landowning families, I frequently encountered individuals whose wives were the daughters of their mother's brother and their father's sister, while they themselves were the offspring of parents whose spouses had been first cousins (though not always double first cousins). This rate of repeated, close cousin marriage may well bring an increase in the risk of congenital abnormalities in the offspring from such unions (Shaw 2009, 2011), but it also results in children whose loyalties are distributed across rival households. When Pakistanis invoke marriage as a proven mechanism for dealing with serious disputes, as they do in the so-called tribal areas of Pakistan, they are not delusional optimists, but have a deep understanding of the complex bonds of mutual obligation that are created through common descent and marital ties. These lineage and marital connections play out overtly in times of conflict. While it is true that much of the conflict that occurs among landowners is directly with those people who share some level of legitimate claim to the land, it is equally true that disputes are not typically resolved in isolation. One needs allies to protect one's land and entering into land disputes invariably means calling on kin members for support.

The actual alliances that emerge from any dispute may nevertheless reflect a complex set of priorities that require careful management and astute political acumen to have a hope of delivering the desired outcomes. The extended period of the land dispute in this northern Punjabi village is not particularly remarkable. Many land disputes can take years to reach some level of temporary resolution. Some erupt into violence that takes a decade or more to get under control. In some extreme cases, individuals may exile themselves from the region after deciding the cost is too high to justify the rewards. I have witnessed older landlords advising young landlords to consider emigrating to another, more peaceful part of the world and beginning life as something other than a Punjabi landlord. The advice is arguably sound, but many young landlords seem unable to follow it.

MARRIAGE AS A TOOL FOR CONFLICT SUPPRESSION

The use of marital alliances to establish peace agreements is certainly not unique to South Asia. The royal families of Europe made good use of strategic marriages between rival households. Such marriages don't so much eliminate conflict and tension, but rather control it. The conflict becomes manageable and over multiple generations can, on occasion fade entirely, though arguably marriage can only ever be part of the conflict management strategy. The many marital alliances that existed across Europe's noble families, appear not, for example, to have effectively suppressed the extreme religious cleavages that led to countless bloody clashes throughout the fifteenth to seventeenth centuries. World War I, similarly, was a war between countries led by close cousins with an intricate network of marital connections (MacMillan 2014). I am not, therefore, trying to suggest that marriages inevitably resolve conflict. Political marriages consolidate and entrench political and social capital within groups. The purpose may be, at times, to minimize conflict, but more typically, it is to restrict inheritance and shore up the relations that form the bedrock of allies in conflict situations. Where marriage is used explicitly to force conflicting parties to cease violent activities, then the conditions for the individuals involved can be brutal. In certain parts of Pakistan, there are marriage arrangements that are knowingly designed to try and stop revenge killings, or blood feuds.

In Punjab, most marriages follow fairly predictable rhetorically approved patterns of like marrying like (Fischer and Finkelstein 1991; Donnan 1988). While there is an easily encountered rhetorical preference for first cousin marriage (either parallel or cross), the reality is that with repeated cousin marriage, more distant cousins are also deemed very good marriages. Marriage within the lineage, or *biradari,* is the least problematic for the division of property, but even *biradari* endogamy doesn't relieve all tension around inheritance. All it means is that land doesn't go *outside* the *biradari.* Given the widespread animosity *within biradaris* it is then unsurprising that cousin marriages do not eliminate all conflict.

Marriages can, however, pave the way for strategic cooperation that does reduce violent conflict, even if they do not eliminate the root causes for the competitive rivalries. In the case above, the absence of a clear male heir led to considerable uncertainty about who should inherit the land. The fact that there was a lot of land, and other assets, meant that this was likely to be a challenging inheritance regardless of the presence or absence of an undisputed heir. The fact is that the feelings of having been deprived at the expense of another, what Foster (1965) called the Image of Limited Good, is a powerful motivator in many circumstances. It isn't only peasant societies that react negatively when one group appears to be benefiting to the detriment of others, but in peasant societies, as Foster and others have noted, it may be easier to observe. In this northern Punjabi village, it is also not entirely without an evidentiary basis. The fact is that all landlords engage in some form of land dispute. Many encroach on their neighbor's land or try to divert water meant for another farmer towards their own crops. Farming is a difficult job and the risk of failure is ever present. When crops fail, whole households suffer. It is therefore entirely predictable and understandable that farmers seek to maximize their own advantage and minimize risk *even* if it has to come at the expense of one of their neighbors. Since we don't exist in the original generation, we also have a long, complicated historical narrative about how others have benefited by taking something away from *our* ancestors. This means that it may not even seem unfair or unjust to take land by force, if one has a household narrative that the parcel of land was *originally* stolen away from its rightful owner. In the early 2000s, there was a spate of robberies from wealthy houses in the North East of England. When they finally caught the man responsible, he denied that he had committed any crime. He argued that all of the wealth that went into those houses was the result of theft from ordinary working people in England and he was simply taking back some of what had been stolen from his ancestors. He was, of course, referring back to a long history of land enclosures, and dispossession from natural resources. I only heard his argument second hand, but he sounded like a working class man who had read a good deal of Marx and Engels and had fully embraced the notion of private property as theft. So we mustn't indulge in thinking that Punjabi peasants are somehow *more* prone to resenting the successes of their neighbors and cousins. Such resentment is alive and well in many parts of the contemporary world, including Britain.

THE NEED FOR CONSTANT MAINTENANCE

One of the striking features of the 2011 land dispute in the Punjabi village was the extent to which conflict must continuously be managed. I have made the case that conflict in Punjab isn't *resolved*, but rather it's *managed*. The reasons for conflict don't go away following a *jirga* but the threat of violence recedes. That is an important outcome for communities, so this is not a rebuke of customary conflict management systems, but it does underscore the need to reject teleological arguments that societies strive for some ideal state of harmony. Conflicts can and do erupt repeatedly. Peace requires as much maintenance as conflict, perhaps more because it can be decidedly challenging to keep factions close and cooperating in the absence of a common threat or enemy.

In the 1920s, when the two Maliks arranged a marriage between historically divided branches of the family, it is likely that they envisaged it as the start of a series of repeated exchanges between the households. One marriage paves the way for future marriages and it is in fact through repeated marital exchanges between households that trust and cooperation can flourish. Such repeated exchange also, paradoxically, paves the way for future conflict through reinforcing the potential rival claims to the same immovable assets. Marriage alone cannot therefore keep violent conflict at bay. It is one part of a complex system of social relations that enable a fulfilment of needs along with rules for inheritance. Both of these are, in turn, impacted by religious structures that are themselves composite sets of ritual and symbolic practices and beliefs.

Prior to the spread of Islamic inheritance rules, the issue of female inheritance of land hardly existed. To be fair, women have been known to inherit land in Punjab, but it was not rhetorically salient in northern Punjab two generations ago. Going back slightly further, the issue of equal inheritance among all male heirs was also irrelevant. At the start of the 19th century, most inheritance in northern Punjab went to a single male heir, usually the eldest son. In the genealogy that I was given access to in the late 1990s from the *shahjrah nasib* carefully curated by my landlord friends, the only information recorded was the name of the heir to the land. It was, therefore, mostly a chain of male names with one per generation. On occasion, there were two or three names in a single generation. When I asked why sometimes brothers were included, I was told that this probably meant they had divided the land, but maybe for some other reason. Perhaps they were spiritually important. The shrine on the mountain just outside the village, for example, is said to be the tomb of an ancestor of the local landlord family. He turned up in the genealogy as a second brother in a single generation. This, I was told, might be because he didn't inherit any land, but he was a saint and so they didn't want to drop him off the genealogy. The key to that genealogy was not principally about recording who was in the family, but rather, who inherited the land[4].

When the practice of dividing land among all surviving male heirs entered into the village, it apparently led to some divisions between the *Upper Walé* and *Niché Walé* Maliks. Those who adopted equal division among all sons appear to have dealt with the potential conflicts introduced by allowing multiple rival claimants to the same land by restricting access to within the narrow *biradari*. Those who continued with primogeniture inheritance could, in contrast, afford to draw their marriage partners from beyond the *biradari*, safe in the knowledge that the land was not open for inheritance outside the restricted lineage group. By reducing the division between the factions of the village, the landlord households then had to deal with the resultant mismatch in inheritance expectations. The conflicts in the 1970s, by all accounts, were rooted in the incompatibility of those expectations.

By the time I first arrived in the village, everyone had accepted equal inheritance among all male heirs, but there was still no talk of including women in land inheritance. When I enquired about female land inheritance I was told that women received their inheritance pre-mortem in the form of generous dowries. Even at the time, that seemed a weak argument, but I had heard the same thing in Lahore more than a decade before, so I accepted that at least some people believed this was a reasonable allocation of household wealth across generations. Less than a decade after I completed my doctoral field research, however, it was clear that there had been substantial changes in the village, as there had been in the country. Pakistan changed between 2000 and 2010 and while I can see the legacy of the old Pakistan, there is no doubt in my mind that some fundamental social structures have been so stressed as to render them effectively extinct except in the minds of men my age or older and in the rapidly aging pages of ethnographies that attempted to represent particular places and times. A number of things led to the changes in Pakistani society. In 1998, I was told by many landlords that educating girls and poor peasants would lead to disruption in society and would only cause everyone to be unhappy. By 2007, some of the very same men who had insisted that girls shouldn't be educated were supporting their daughters to pursue university education, including postgraduate degrees. Shi'a Muslims used to stand out for the reverence with which they treated education for both boys and girls. These days, many Barelvi Sunni Muslims share that fervor for ensuring that all of their children, boys and girls, are given the chance to attain the highest educational qualifications possible.

Extending land inheritance and education to a wider pool of the population has led to disruption, as my friends in the late 1990s forewarned, and has no doubt made some people unhappy. Land disputes include women now in ways that would have been hard to imagine two generations ago. Women were always involved and important, but now they are leaders in the disputes. Husbands, on behalf of their wives, can make inheritance claims in order to protect their children's future assets. Where marriages have occurred outside the *biradari,* this has inevitably forced landlord families to contemplate family land falling under the control of people who do not share their common stake in the collective honor or reputation of the lineage group. Minimizing the consequences of such disconnected interests is something that requires careful maintenance. Repeated marriages between the out-group, can eventually lead to a shifting of the "hard" boundary of insider/outsider. But of course, as noted above, the enmity within the family boundaries isn't necessarily trivial. Consequently, the downside of transforming one's outside marriage exchange partner into an insider group is that the potential for *sharika* or *tarburwali* is still present, but the benefits of bringing in the diversity of expertise, knowledge and networks diminishes with each repeated marriage exchange.

THE COST-BENEFIT ANALYSIS OF MARRYING OUT

Marriage is challenging either endogamously or exogamously. The implications of every union must be weighed up carefully. Households bear the brunt of problems should they arise, hence, the ubiquitous uninvited offers of advice from relatives. The right combination of *endo* and *exo* marriages can provide the necessary robustness to ensure the reproduction of the agnatic corporate group, in this case the *biradari,* while still creating bridging ties to other *biradari* to develop the critical support network to infuse sufficient resilience to adapt to major shocks and instability.

I used a specific extended conflict to illustrate the challenges facing landowning families in rural Pakistan. It might seem to serve as something of a cautionary tale about the limits of trying to use marriage to maintain *status quo* positions. The family at the heart of the conflict has managed their marriages to deal with being a minority landowning *biradari* in a turbulent region with unreliable agricultural resources (principally rain). They survived the historical waves of invading armies, the rise and fall of the British Raj, the creation of Pakistan and its volatile state politics, but in the absence of a clear male heir, the family was brought to a standstill for several years. To be sure, life continued alongside the serious disputes. Agriculture continued and to some extent, it might be seen as a productive period in the family's history because individual members actively sought allies from outside the *biradari,* the village and the region. The family has long been involved in the wings of state politics, but historically through only a select minority of prominent family leaders. During this conflict period, more individuals sought out the support of prominent political leaders in the area and forged relationships of varying strength with most political party activists in the area.

Many of the disputants drew on affinal links outside of the close *biradari*. It was in this period, in fact, that I came to develop a more sophisticated understanding of the difference between *rishtadar* (related people) and *biradari* (lineage relatives). When I first worked in the area, I heard the term *rishta* and knew that it meant some type of extended family. *Biradari,* on the other hand, clearly meant family that shared a common male ancestor. Both were suitable pools of people for arranging marriages, but one generated more implications of *sharika* than the other. Unsurprisingly, during the period of heightened conflict between close cousins (*sharik*), the *rishta* became more important. Perhaps it was a coincidence, but shortly before the serious conflict erupted, there had been another important marriage union between two distant branches of the family who had not, in the late 1990s, been referred to as falling within the same *biradari*. By 2012/2013, the visits between the hitherto distant relatives in from villages outside the immediate sphere of influence of local landlords had increased considerably. There were a new set of young grandchildren present in the house and that seemed to be the stated cause for the visits back and forth. I wouldn't under estimate that as a genuine motivator for the visits, rural Pakistanis really do seem to love spending time with small children without any ulterior motives, but as it happens, the visits were also opportunities to try and repair the damage between the conflicting households in the village. These "external" *rishta* appeared to be able to move more freely between the factions and either calm troubled waters or at least keep information flowing. I found myself in a similar position, but was far too naïve and inexperienced to be able to make any useful contribution. I could move from faction to faction and learn more about the conflict, but I was completely incapable of being "useful" to anyone but myself. The presence of external *mehram* people, who were trusted to move in private family areas, served an important function in keeping life going in what might otherwise have descended into the stalemate described by Frembgen (2014) or Keiser (1991) in the tribal areas of Pakistan.

NOTES

1. One of my personal favorites from these sweeping assessments of different castes comes from a *Gazetteer* originally published in 1930 about Gujars, "Their proneness to quarrelling and intriguing are blots on their character, but not much more evil can be said of them." (*Gazetteer of the Attock District* 2003, 111) Needless to say, they do not appear to be more prone to quarrelling and intriguing than their neighbors. I also admit, that since I am particularly interested in both of these activities, perhaps

people share more stories about these things with me than were I to be more narrowly interested in other topics.

2. It may be that a landlord class emerges as one possible adaptation to minimize the risks of significant crop failure, which unfortunately happens reasonably frequently when the only source of irrigation is rain.

3. Historically, this office oversaw revenue collection on behalf of the state and retained a percentage of the collection as compensation. While the powers of the *numberdar* have changed in post independence Pakistan, the office continues to be both materially and symbolically important.

4. The landowners of Punjab appear to have been particularly active for some time in attempting to control all legislation regulating inheritance, including well before the creation of Pakistan. The Unionist Party, a political organization known for supporting both the British Raj and the interests of large landowners, held a heated debate in 1931 about the seeming contradiction of their land inheritance practices and *shari'a* laws. Unsurprisingly, they decided that primogeniture inheritance was compatible with "tribal" custom and therefore legitimate. Gilmartin (1988) argues that these debates were largely symbolic because the rights of large landowners were enshrined in various pieces of legislation, but they allowed key landowners to assert their "tribal" legitimacy to contest those who invoked Islam as a challenge to both the British and those who supported them.

Chapter 6

Landed Elite

I have looked for cultural patterns throughout my research on Pakistan. This has led me to see continuity across boundary lines that are culturally meaningful on the ground according to many local people. One of the oft-repeated assertions in urban Pakistan involves strong declarations about the differences between urban and rural Pakistan. Not only do I find this a difficult distinction to sustain empirically, I find it decidedly unhelpful in making sense of some critical cultural practices in ostensibly modern social institutions. In this chapter, I turn my attention to some of the regional dynastic political networks and the ways in which individuals act as representatives of clusters of interests—both those directly tied to their dynastic group as well as others. The dynasties serve to reinforce existing distributions of power and resources including for rival dynasties. Party politics across South Asia exhibits remarkable evidence of dynastic transmission of authority and control. While there are clearly advantages to restricting potential party leaders in terms of reducing the disruption of leadership contests, this necessarily limits the extent to which parties are able to shift and respond to changes in the political landscape. The Bhuttos are perhaps the most famous contemporary Pakistani political dynasty, but dynastic trends have impacted the shape of Pakistan's provincial and national party politics since independence. As with the other chapters, this chapter combines ethnographic evidence from across Pakistan with primary ethnographic material produced in northern and central Punjab to show the ways in which the predictability provided by ascribing charisma and expertise to the offspring of influential leaders can reduce instability while simultaneously retarding the development of effective participatory democratic social institutions.

Ultimately, anthropological analyses must be tested against empirical data. It's important to carry out thought experiments and philosophical boundary stretching, but anthropology is at its heart, an empirical extension of the natural sciences. It isn't a natural science like the others, because we understand ourselves differently from how we understand the rest of the natural world. That means that we are very much part of the subject of analysis and that makes it difficult to rely on exactly the same methods and theories that we use to understand nonhuman phenomena. Consequently, we've had to develop a distinct branch of the natural sciences to study ourselves and our relationship to the rest of the world. Partly, that involves our imagination. We need to dream up questions and ways of producing data that might help us answer those questions. Within anthropology, kinship is one of those subfields that has become highly elaborated and from which a number of methods and theories have emerged. Some of them have been abandoned because when applied to the empirical record, they fell short of what was needed. All of them have been updated and amended as a result of application to the empirical data. We produce ethnographic accounts using methods and as those methods are modified, we begin to understand our data in different ways. That can, on occasion, lead us to revisiting the credibility of data produced using earlier methods. Thus far, I've largely focused on traditional subject matter for anthropology. Some might call it old fashioned anthropology. Using marriage records as the basis for generating network data in a village is something that any anthropologist from the past century might do—though obviously not necessarily with the software assistance or in pursuit of the same questions. Examining processes of conflict at the local level over land, people and movable resources, is part and parcel of what anthropologists have done since at least the time of Sir Henry Maine (1861). Here I extend the old-fashioned focus on village and regional-level actors to include state actors more explicitly. This has not only become relatively common in political anthropology, it has arguably become unavoidable in most contexts. There are certainly cases in which the role of the state and its actors may be less relevant, and therefore appear more muted, or even silent in some ethnographic accounts, but they must be fewer and farther between than at any point in the history of anthropology. One of the things that makes kinship so relevant for the ethnography of Pakistan is precisely the extent to which studies of local level social organization and practices can be used to make sense of larger scale social institutions and relations.

ARISTOCRATIC FAMILIES

The examples presented in this chapter are of families that derive some part of their prestige and power from historical land ownership. There are numerous examples of historically powerful families that have persisted for several hundred years. The so-called princely estates held different statuses under different regimes, and some of them enjoyed considerable autonomy. As I explained in chapter 3, on the historical turbulence of India, powerful regimes, such as the Mughals, adopted a variety of strategies to subordinate the independent aristocratic regimes, including hostage taking and coerced marriage with the daughters of the leaders. In post Partition Pakistan, the legacy of these landed elites has been fiercely protective of their positions. The Punjab Unionist Party, in the decades leading up to independence and Partition, worked closely with the British and developed institutional mechanisms for retaining control over both the material and symbolic resources of the province. In contrast to these rather conservative defenders of the *status quo*, the students of Aligarh University were the cream of the crop of Muslim leadership in India and the principle organizers of the Indian Muslim League and the architects of a separate homeland for Indian Muslims. When these Mumbai- and Dhaka-based Muslim League leaders crossed over the border to assume control over Pakistan, I suspect they didn't appreciate just how creative and tenacious the local landowners could be. In 1968, Mahbub ul Haq claimed that there were just 22 families who controlled the bulk of the resources in the country, and it is a safe bet he was principally referring to these well entrenched landed elite families (see Lyon and Mughal 2016). Although he declined to provide the actual list and there are many "versions" of who actually might be included, the fundamental recognition that some families exercised disproportionate power in relation to the vast majority was, and is, undoubtedly true.

I have spent over two decades working with and learning from representatives of this landed elite class. Unlike some people who have worked with them, I have found them to be understandable and relatable. I am neither blind to their flaws, nor do I condone all of their actions, yet I would be a hypocrite if I said that I was certain I would not act as they do, were I to have been born into their families. The turbulence that I have tried to describe in my published work on northern Punjab is undeniable. The consequences of political incompetence or naïve idealism can be devastating. Protecting one's resources, both material and symbolic, is not an idle activity in rural Pakistan. Whether one has seen the disenfranchisement of a former landowner or not, the specter of formerly "respectable" landowners lurks in all rural areas. Everyone is aware that land must be fought for and protected and can be lost if one doesn't continually and vigilantly police one's position.

Pakistan's landed elite, the so-called aristocracy, has managed to retain control in Pakistan in ways that can be surprising. India's concerted efforts to undermine and ultimately supplant the old princely rulers have resulted in a noticeably different political landscape. To be sure, the old princely rulers can often still wield considerable influence, but the federal state has imposed meaningful constraints on their overt exercise of power. In contrast,

Pakistan's landed elite continue to control substantial parts of the state and have effectively been able to hijack state institutions to extract resources to bolster their own patronage positions in local contexts (see especially Martin 2014, 2016, 2018). The mechanisms for influencing and even subsuming state interests within parochial interests varies, but historically, the landed elite of Pakistan have demonstrated considerable versatility and skill at reproducing their political status (Javid 2011).

This chapter and the next chart some of the ways in which key families have been able to harness their position as landed elite to effect significant control over state electoral institutions. The approach adopted here focuses on Pakistani politics at a level that draws on both political science as well as anthropology. I look at the role of lineal and marital connections that characterize and influence the way that Pakistani electoral politics take place. This is not to deny the democratic structures of institutions in Pakistan or to suggest that because of marriage networks they are less robust or democratic than other countries. They may be, but not *because* of kinship. Reliance on kinship relations is an attempt to counter Pakistan's electoral problems, rather than the cause of them. This may be a contentious statement. However, one of the goals of this book is to demonstrate that political kinship is not the villain of the Pakistani state, but a logical work around for a state that, like all states, has some fundamental flaws and lacks the resources of many other states to compensate bureaucratically for them.

Dynasties have been notoriously important in post-independence South Asian states. India has had its national and regional dynastic families such as the Nehrus, with multiple prime ministers and numerous members of parliament (Jaffrelot 2006). These have included men and women and extended to in-marrying members from different lineages (and countries) as place holders for the rising next generation of leaders to emerge. Bangladesh, similarly, has a history not only of descent based dynasties, but of widows taking over following their husbands' untimely violent deaths. Pakistan's dynasties reflect the distribution of power brokers across the country. The dynastic groupings are associated with specific regions of the country and while there are many strategic alliances, they have also exhibited considerable tensions in their attempts to shift control away from one another.

I do not include here the short-lived but unfulfilled dynastic legacy of the man credited with leading the creation of Pakistan, the Quaid-i-Azam (Great Leader) Mohammad Ali Jinnah, but it is worth noting that his sister, Fatima Jinnah, ran a very competitive, though ultimately unsuccessful bid for the office of president against the military general, Ayub Khan in 1965. Fatima Jinnah was the leader of the opposition against Ayub Khan and was a vocal advocate for civil rights. Since her demise in 1967, however, there have been no other claimants to the Jinnah mantle.

Just to give a sense of how pervasive lineage connections are between elected office holders in Pakistan, I show an anonymized network map of the elected officials from the 2013 elections separated by shared lineage membership (see figure 6.1). This map includes all Members of the National Assembly, the Punjab Provincial Assembly and the District officials from a random sample of Districts that I happen to have spent some time in. It is, of course, not a complete network, because it *only* includes those individuals who hold office and leaves out all of the connections to people who do not hold any elected office that connect these lineages.

This isn't as bad as some network spaghetti bowls, but it's not exactly easy to make out what's going on, other than the fact that there are a few lineage groups that seem to have been very successful in the 2013 elections. When the lineages are collapsed into a single node, to simplify visual interpretation, there remain a small number of links between the lineages through marriage (see figure 6.2). While there aren't many of these direct marriage links between actual office holders, they represent a potentially powerful bloc building tool within the elected bodies.

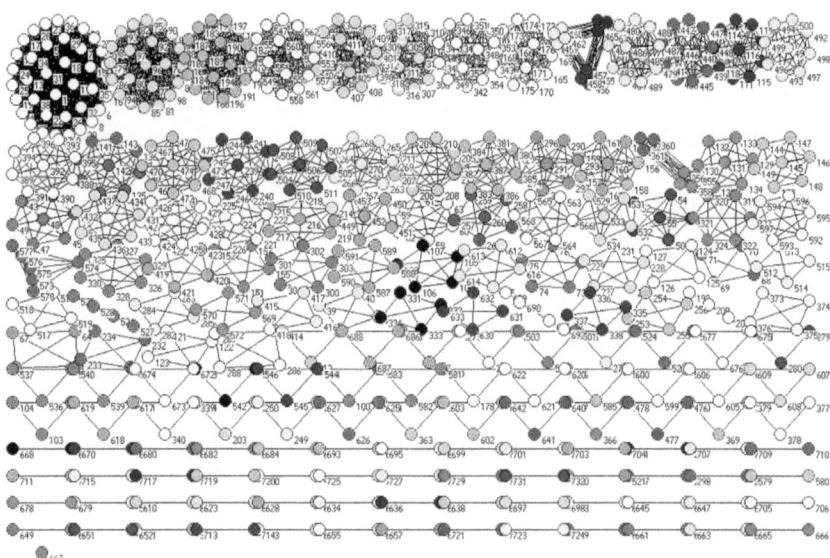

Figure 6.1 Network Map of Elected Officials from the 2013 Elections. Total = 732 / MNA = 342 / Punjab Provincial Assembly = 371 / Other elected officials = 19. I am extremely grateful to Flavia Cahn, who acted as an exemplary summer intern one summer during her undergraduate studies to extract a substantial part of these data from a special issue of *The Herald* (see good summaries of the data in Cheema, Javid, and Naseer 2013; Zahid 2013) and enter it into a form that could be processed computationally. *Source*: Author generated graph.

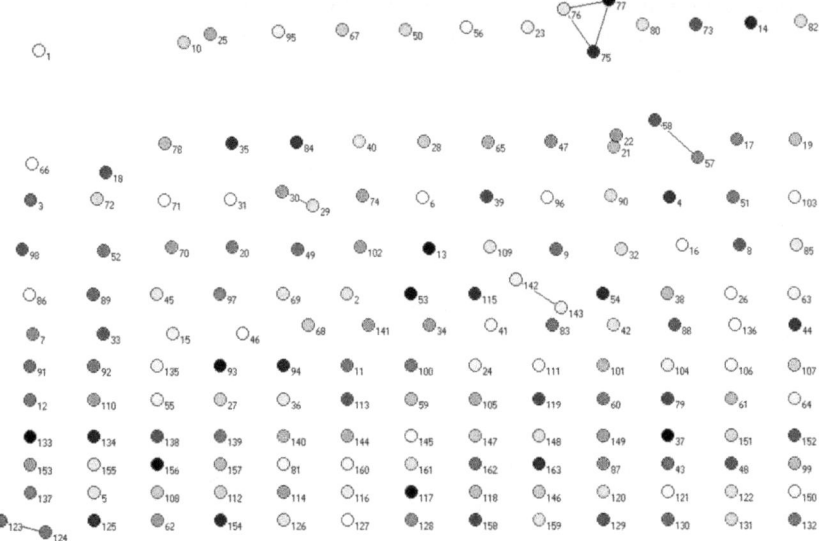

Figure 6.2 Elected Officials from the 2013 Elections with Lineages Collapsed. Links between nodes are marital links. *Source*: Author generated graph.

The big picture certainly suggests that dynasties of lineage and marriage are worth paying attention to in Pakistani electoral politics. While there are different ways of analyzing these data, it helps to have a sense of who these people are and just how different kinship networks are able to leverage the combined impact of descent and affinal connections. In this chapter and the next, I examine several case studies of kinship networks to illustrate the complexity of interconnections *between* the dynasties. These case studies are not fire-gapped families, to be sure. Distinct kinship networks can and do connect either through descent or marriage, but even when that isn't the case, there are bonds of friendship and shared financial interest that mean that the cases I focus on in this and the next chapter should not be treated as if they are isolated from one another. Both genealogical and network analyses provide powerful entry points for making sense of complex communities, but there can be issues of completeness. At what point can we meaningfully *stop* eliciting relationship data and say we have a whole network or genealogy. We know that if are prepared to go back just a few generations, it can be possible to find lineage connections between people who have no known relationship in the present,[1] but operating at the usual field-working level of an anthropologist, I prioritized connections that were likely to be culturally meaningful to contemporary people. I set aside concerns about looking for possibly more obscure connections either historical or other, and instead focused on the public links that bind each of these ostensibly distinct lineage dynasties to other dynasties via marriage.

The following cases illustrate some critical aspects of managing electoral success in Pakistani politics. They each represent a different solution to the problem of having to harness support across large parts of the country. The first example, from Punjab, demonstrates the power of linking many regionally distinct networks. The *national* party is actually an emergent property of distinct regional power networks that may share few ideological manifesto goals. While this kind of network of networks can and does produce electoral success, it struggles to deliver a coherent political vision that can transcend local priorities. The second example illustrates the power of the super landowners. My own experience is with relatively modest landowners who own, at most, thousands of hectares and command similar numbers of peasant farmers and their families. In certain parts of Pakistan, however, there are mega landowners who control many tens of thousands of hectares and can command many tens of thousands of peasant farmers. These mega landowners are reputed to have private armies, run their own prison systems and effectively operate parallel states within the country. It is not unusual to hear them accused of perpetuating slavery because they have effective control over all the material resources required to survive and are said to strictly control the movement of the peasants who live on their property. The example I illustrate in this chapter comes from Sindh, and while I think it is entirely inappropriate to assert that the Bhuttos either perpetuate or condone slavery, they serve an important example of how a very large landowning family has managed to secure a place in the political history of pre and post Partition Pakistan and India. Much like the more modest landowners with whom I am more familiar, they appear to have adopted strategic marital alliances to consolidate and bridge their influence. Unlike the first example, of a network of networks, they are seemingly not as dependent on drawing on the networked influence of other regional power networks. The striking example of bridging that I demonstrate here, between a Sindhi and a Balochi, illustrates that marriages may potentially provide substantial networking advantages, they do not necessarily confer straightforward electoral advantage. In the case of the Bhuttos, the significant political success has been firmly established for many generations. The political success of the Zardaris, on the other hand, seems clearly to be a direct consequence of the marital connection. Complicating matters, the lack of electoral success in recent elections of Zardari-Bhutto underscores the importance of understanding marital alliances in conjunction with both descent transmission *and* other types of network loyalties.

PEDIGREES AND NETWORKS

I have provided both a partial genealogical, or pedigree, record for the families along with a network cluster graph to illustrate the extent to which marriage *joins* networks of regionally important families. The network cluster graphs are generated from the centrality measurements of the nodes. Nodes that share common links to other nodes are potentially included within the same cluster. In the cases presented here, each descent group inevitably falls within a common cluster because there are many overlapping links between the individual members. The marriages that link these clusters illustrate the bridging potential across distinct descent groups, that also happen to be distributed geographically around the country. Within each of the clusters, there is at least one, and usually more, elected politician. I have removed the names from the cluster graphs because the point is not to identify individual players, but rather to demonstrate the pattern of using marriages to bridge significant clusters of powerful people who would otherwise have no obvious direct connection to one another.

THE CHAUDHRYS OF GUJERAT AND REGIONAL LINKS

I have written about the incredible Chaudhrys of Gujerat elsewhere (Lyon and Mughal 2016). They demonstrate the significance of networks as clearly as any political bloc. The networks that they've created since the 1950s are demonstrably influential at both provincial and national levels. Their members have held high political offices and been instrumental in shaping the political decisions of successive governments. Starting from a modest beginning in post Partition politics, the founder of this dynasty, Chaudhry Zahoor Elahi, rose to prominence in the 1950s. He held a variety of offices before his assassination in 1981 and while some may disagree with his politics, none can question his courage in standing up to the powerful of Pakistan. In the 1960s, he opposed the military president, Ayub Khan, and then in the 1970s, he opposed Z.A. Bhutto's government. He was jailed by Z.A. Bhutto's government in the 1970s and ultimately met an untimely violent death. His elder brother, Chaudhry Manzoor Elahi, devoted himself to running the family business.

Chaudhry Zahoor Elahi's sons have been extraordinarily successful in Pakistani politics. His eldest, Chaudhry Shujaat Hussain, was a federal minister multiple times. Chaudhry Wajahat Hussain, one of his younger sons, was a member of the National Assembly and federal minister between 2002 and 2013. The third brother, Chaudhry Shafaat Hussain, was a district nazim (the former chief executive at the district level prior to reforms implemented in 2010). His daughters are equally significant in maintaining the family's considerable influence, despite only rarely standing for elected office (Butt 2016).

The marriage networks of the Chaudhrys are convoluted and exciting enough to be the stuff of fiction. They have strategically allied themselves with powerful families across Punjab and Khyber-Pukhtunhwa and while we will never know the private conversations between the members of these families, it is fascinating to speculate what deals may have been struck at family weddings and funerals in Mianwali, Gujerat, Hazara, and Attock. It is certainly interesting that while there have been arguments between and within these "families," they regularly find themselves on the same side of contentious political battles.

One of the most impressive aspects of the Chaudhry marital network is its geographical distribution. Without casting any aspersions on the family, it is uncanny how they have managed to bind together key districts in Punjab and Khyber-Pukhtunkhwa through marriage arrangements. The marriage connections certainly don't guarantee that there is political cooperation and harmony at all times, but it provides a critical mechanism for merging social and political relationships of strategic cooperation. In the 2018 elections, for example, members of the complex marriage network did not all join Imran Khan's winning PTI party, however, they strategically supported one another in the 2018 elections (a move designed to prevent either a PML-N or PPP majority). Following the July elections, PML-Q, under Chaudhry Shujaat Hussain's leadership, formally supported PTI's efforts to form a government in Punjab.

The marriage network of the Gujerati Chaudhrys links them to a number of regionally influential families around Punjab and Khyber-Pukhtunkhwa. One of these is based in Attock District, in the region in which I have conducted field research for more than two decades. I have had the opportunity to observe this political family from afar for some time. I admit to being somewhat partisan when it comes to Attock. My friends in the region are heavily invested in local politics and care deeply about the outcomes of elections. Following elections, they are directly impacted by the ways in which state resources are utilized before the next election or coup. The landlords with whom I have worked are preoccupied with the serious agricultural challenges that come from operating in a rain fed region. They have developed underground water extraction, but this comes at a high environmental and economic cost. They are, as I've said elsewhere (Lyon 2004), a minority *qaum* of Gujars, surrounded by villages controlled by another minority *qaum* of Khattars. The Gujars are numerous as peasant farmers, but don't control many villages, so as landlords, they are locally a minority. The Khattars, in contrast, are a minority everywhere, but as landlords, control a large number of villages in the area. The Gujar landlords are aware that good relations with their Khattar neighbors have been critical for their continued ownership and control of their lands. Consequently, their political allegiances have largely been aligned with the dominant Khattar families. This has been brought about not through marriage, which is discouraged across *qaum* boundaries, but through strategic friendships and support during political elections. The Khattars are in a position to win electoral politics largely through these sorts of strategic alliances. They have strong marital networks that consolidate their support across different political allegiances. One of the most successful politicians from Attock provides an illustrative example of how the right marriages can ensure durable alliances through the volatile changes in the political landscape at the national level.

Major Tahir Sadiq is the current leader of the Khattar political "machine" from Attock District. Both his father and mother were members of the Punjab Provincial Assembly. His mother took over her husband's seat when he died. Major Sahib, as he is affectionately and respectfully called by local people, has held a variety of elected positions. Both his son, Zain Elahi, and daughter, Eman Tahir,[2] have also successfully won elected positions. Undoubtedly one key to Major Sahib's success is his marital links to one of the most successful political families in Punjab. His wife comes from the extremely influential Chaudhry family from Gujerat.[3]

Major Tahir Sadiq's political bloc is a good case study for understanding the fluidity of regional Pakistani politics. It is not simply a subsidiary of the more nationally prominent political network of the Chaudhrys of Gujerat, but operates independently and clearly has divergent interests at times. In the 1990s, Major Sahib held office in the Punjab Provincial Assembly with the PML. He was ostensibly a supporter of the then prime minister, Mian Nawaz Sharif but had very close ties to his brother-in-law, who was a rival for leadership within the PML and who later went on to lead his own faction of the PML that supported General Musharraf's military regime, the so called Qauf league. At that time, most of the major positions in Attock District were held by PML candidates, but there was identifiable support for the People's Party of Pakistan (PPP) as well. Other parties were hardly present in Attock at the time. The military coup of General Musharraf led to a more open split within the PML into multiple groups. One part supported the exiled former prime minister, Nawaz Sharif who formed his own named faction of PML following his ouster from office in 1999, adopting the letter N after the party name (PML-N) to indicate affiliation with Nawaz. Other PML supporters threw their weight behind the military under the leadership of Chaudhry Shujaat Hussain and adopted the letter Q as their identifier, suggesting an affinity with the founding leader of Pakistan, the Quaid-i-Azam, Mohammad Ali Jinnah. Major Tahir Sadiq made the necessary shift to openly supporting PML-Q and his in-laws, the Chaudhrys of Gujerat. After the departure of General Musharraf and the collapse of support for the PML-Q, Major Tahir Sadiq became the head of his own, more provincial political bloc, aptly named the Major Tahir Sadiq Group. They ran independently from the major political parties,

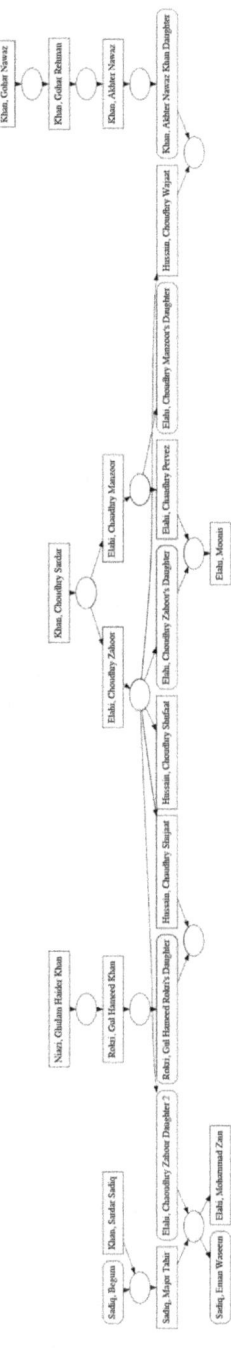

Figure 6.3 The Kinship Network of the Chaudhrys of Gujerat, Including the Influential Attock Family Led by Major Tahir Sadiq. *Source:* Author generated graph.

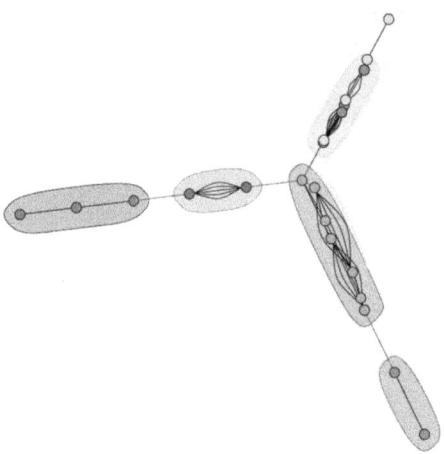

Figure 6.4 The Kinship Network of the Chaudhrys of Gujerat (Including the Cluster Based in Attock). The names have been removed to allow the clusters to stand out. The links between the different clusters is clear. Within each cluster, there is at least one prominent politician. *Source*: Author generated graph.

but people on the ground assured me that he was still very close to PML-Q and the Army.

Major Tahir Sadiq does not appear to be primarily interested in his own land disputes.[4] He has amassed enough land and wealth that his focus is on political power at the provincial and regional levels. He does not appear to have national or international political ambitions, but unlike the landlords with whom I work more closely, his horizon extends well beyond protecting his own patch.

THE BHUTTOS

The Bhuttos are one of the most famous political families of Pakistan. Before Pakistan existed, the Bhuttos were successful politicians in British India. The founder of one of Pakistan's most successful political parties, the People's Party of Pakistan (PPP), Zulfikar Ali Bhutto, expanded his family's dynastic success in ways that continue to influence the direction of both Sindh and Pakistan, despite the tragic assassination of many of its key members. Z.A. Bhutto was executed by General Zia ul Haq, the military general who led the coup that removed him from office in 1977. The details of the execution remain contested, but everyone agrees that his body was hanged in 1979 in an unprecedented governmental act. Hitherto, the political elite of Pakistan had been subjected to violent assassination, but had managed to avoid state sanctioned execution.

Landed Elite 93

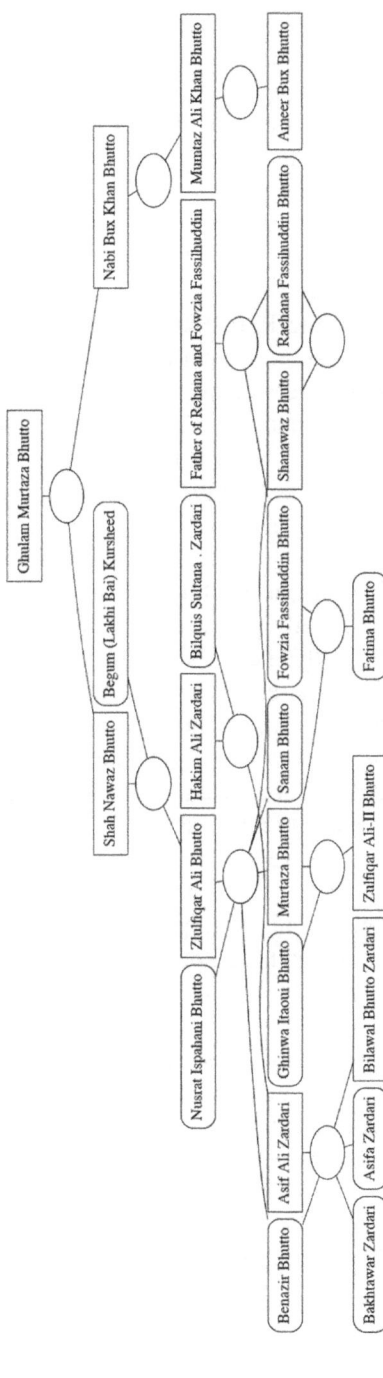

Figure 6.5 The Bhutto Kinship Network. The Bhutto family has been prominent in Sindhi politics since the 19th century. The marriage between the Bhuttos and the Zardaris brought together two powerful landlord families in Sindh and Balochistan. *Source:* Author generated graph.

The children of Z.A. Bhutto have found themselves the victims of violence as well. His eldest son was assassinated in mysterious circumstances and the rumors of who ordered the act are as wild as they are widespread. In 2007, Benazir Bhutto, the former prime minister, was assassinated in the same park in Rawalpindi that was the site of the assassination of Pakistan's first prime minister, Liaqat Ali Khan. As with her brother, there are numerous conspiracy theories about who might be both directly and indirectly responsible for her violent death. Z.A. Bhutto's youngest son, Shahnawaz, was murdered in Europe.[5]

Following the assassination of Benazir Bhutto, her husband, Asif Ali Zardari, assumed leadership of the PPP. Her son, Bilawal Bhutto Zardari, 21 years old at the time, became the formal chairman of the PPP. He was still studying in the UK so his direct involvement in Pakistani politics was somewhat restricted, but his presence was symbolically important for the continuation of the Bhutto legacy. This was not without some contestation, of course. Bilawal was not known as Bhutto Zardari prior to the death of his mother. That attribution was hastily introduced to secure his legitimacy as the heir to the Bhutto Dynasty. In fact, following the logic of dominant notions of conception, he is arguably *not* the legitimate heir to the Bhutto mantle. Patrilineal inheritance is rhetorically powerful in Pakistan. This is justified both religiously and sociologically. People cite the sayings of the Prophet, who is supposed to have said that mothers are the "vessel" into which fathers "pour their milk" (see chapter 4: Descent, Marriage, and Building Networks). As vessels, mothers are important nurturing elements in children's lives, but are not able to transmit essential substance that comes from the father's lineage. This essential substance is known as *nasl*. *Nasl* shapes a person in ways that will apparently emerge regardless of the nurturing environment in which a person grows up and lives. By this logic, Bilawal is a Zardari, rather than a Bhutto. And while that is an important political family in Sindh and Balochistan, it isn't a name that holds, or held, significant political clout nationally in the way that Bhutto does. This may help explain why Bilawal, despite demonstrating considerable courage and substantially developing his political sophistication since the death of his mother, lost his election in 2018 and has not thus far managed to live up to the expectations and hopes of his supporters. He is still very young for a politician in Pakistan (born in 1988), so his reliance on a contentious lineage connection coupled with the absence of a strategic marital partner is only part of his problem. The perception of inexperience may be a greater challenge, for the time being.

Perhaps when Bilawal Bhutto Zardari does get married, his affinal connections may alter his electoral fortunes. He has apparently received numerous marriage proposals. He has publicly stated on more than one occasion that any woman he chooses to marry must first be approved by his two sisters[6]

(*The Economic Times* 2016). While this falls somewhat outside the scope of the current argument, it is interesting to note that he has been so demonstrative in his trust for his sisters. Once again, I find it striking that a society so overtly masculine in many ways and that goes to such great lengths to segregate genders, seems to depend enormously on the cooperative presence of men and women. Perhaps one of the lesser known secrets of Pakistan is just how important and influential women really are (see Lyon 2017 for a discussion of brother-sister relations in Pakistan).

THE LIMITATIONS OF MARRIAGE

Marriage in the examples I present in this chapter and the next are crucial examples of *how* to connect networks of networks. It does not guarantee, nor does it even appear to make more likely, political or ideological *agreement between* those networks. Instead, it establishes networks of mutual self-interest in which the different blocs will support one another so long as their own self-interest is not compromised. When Major Tahir Sadiq switched political parties over the years, he was perhaps not motivated by a change in political manifesto attachment, but rather a sustained and committed loyalty to protecting the interests of landed elites in his part of Punjab. The fact that this motive aligns well with prominent landowners in Gujerat, Mianwali, Hazara, and other Punjabi Districts, means that in a sense, like their Unionist Party forebears, they did share something akin to a meaningful political agenda. It's just not one that would necessarily win the support of landless peasant voters, were they to spend much time scrutinizing it.

In the next chapter, which serves as a companion to this one, I turn my attention to the rivals of the landed elite in the country: Nawaz Sharif and Imran Khan. Nawaz Sharif is arguably one of the most successful politicians in Pakistan's history, and yet he has been removed from office forcibly on multiple occasions and has spent many years both in exile and in prison. Unlike the families discussed in this chapter, his wealth has been generated from industrial activities. While he certainly owns land, his power base is urban and is not predicated on the remnants of the traditional sharecropping and *jajman* systems that were pervasive across modern-day Pakistan for centuries. It may seem unusual for me to include Imran Khan as a nontraditional, non-landowning elite. This is not because he and his family don't own considerable land, but rather because his authority isn't fundamentally rooted in his traditional position as a landowning Khan. His celebrity status as a cricket star thrust him into the public consciousness in a way that few other politicians can even imagine. His subsequent political crusade against corruption persisted for many years with little to no widespread political success despite his family status. He, like Nawaz Sharif, therefore had to establish a different route to electoral success than the Bhuttos and the Chaudhrys. Nevertheless, just like the landed elite, it will become clear the extent to which electoral success in Pakistan *demands* coalitions of distinct power bases. In other words, no single party or family can win Pakistani elections on their own. Even when it may look like a single political party has dominated the electoral landscape, they are in fact the visible face of a complex collection of separate power networks all driven by a *realpolitik* of parochial self-interest. Marriage is certainly not the only mechanism for building such coalitions, but it appears to be a particularly successful one in Pakistan.

NOTES

1. For example, Barack Obama and Dick Cheney are apparently eighth cousins "Lynne Cheney: VP, Obama Are Eighth Cousins," *NBC News*, 2007, http://www.nbcnews.com/id/21340764/ns/politics/t/lynne-cheney-vp-obama-are-eighth-cousins/#.XB1zEs_7TOQ.

2. Sometimes called Eman Waseem.

3. I was told by many of his local supporters that his wife was the sister of Chaudhry Shujaat Hussain, but newspapers often report him as the brother-in-law of Pervez Elahi. In practice, there is little distinction between these two since they are *chachazad-bhai,* or patrilateral first cousins. The literal translation of the Urdu kin term is father's brother's offspring-brother.

4. Though I have no doubt that there are people who police his lands very carefully on his behalf.

5. There are rumors that Shahnawaz Bhutto's widow, Raehana Fassilhudin may have been responsible for his death. Whether there is any truth to those rumors or not, Shawnawaz' brother, Murtaza Bhutto, divorced his own wife, Fowzia Fassilhuddin (Raehana's sister) following the assassination of his brother.

6. *The Economic Times*, 2016, "Have Received Several Marriage Proposals: Bilawal Bhutto Zardari," November 6, 2016, https://economictimes.indiatimes.com/magazines/panache/have-received-several-marriage-proposals-bilawal-bhutto-zardari/articleshow/55263663.cms.

Chapter 7

Industrialist and Populist Challengers

Landed elites clearly had advantages from the earliest days of independent Pakistan. For the first 30 years, the state was largely controlled either by the military or the landed elite. The leaders of the Indian Muslim League, who had established the first government of Pakistan as the Pakistan Muslim League, were unable to establish stable governing institutions so that by 1958, the country experienced its first period of direct Martial Law rule under Ayub Khan. The landed elite continued to sway the country and thwart his efforts at democratization and land redistribution. The resistance to Ayub Khan's political initiatives in these areas reveal the impotence of the state at the time. As one large landowner in northern Punjab explained to me, "No one willingly gives up land that their fathers have fought for in the past—not you, and not us. So all these peasants who claim to own land around here, that's nonsense. This land belongs to my family—always has and always will." Slowly, however, rival sources of authority and power have emerged in Pakistan. In the 1980s, the Sharif brothers, Nawaz and Shahbaz, navigated the treacherous state politics under Zia ul Haq to assume formal authority over Punjab province. More recently, the charismatic cricket captain, Imran Khan, has successfully leveraged what had been a one man crusade into a governing party at provincial and national levels. In this chapter, I look at the ways in which an industrialist and a celebrity were able to circumvent the near monopoly of power held by the landed elite for the majority of Pakistan's history. The success of groups whose basis of power comes from something other than land ownership should not be understood as necessarily a revolutionary departure from landed elite dominance, of course. As is clear from the evidence, an important part of the success of these groups has been the extent to which they have been able to secure the support of the landed elites and the military. There is undoubtedly scope for different power bases in Pakistan, but it is hard to imagine how anyone might effectively win elections and govern the state *without* the support of the two crucial interrelated concentrations of power that exist among the landed elite and the military.

THE SHARIFS

The Sharifs may be one of the most interesting political families in Pakistan. Unlike most politically powerful families in Pakistan, the foundation of their status is not land. They were not substantial landowners prior to the creation of Pakistan. They were not, in fact, particularly significant in any way prior to 1947. In some ways, they represent the social mobility that is possible in Pakistan. The Sharif patriarch, Mian Muhammad Sharif, was an industrialist who managed to accumulate substantial wealth through the 1950s and 1960s as one of the founders of the Ittefaq Group. Bhutto's nationalization program in the 1970s hit the Sharifs rather hard and brought home the importance of controlling state political apparatuses. In order to protect himself from future nationalizations and indeed to reclaim what he considered was unfairly confiscated, he placed his sons in political positions. His eldest son, Nawaz Sharif, leveraged his support for the military regime of Zia ul Haq into high profile political offices in Lahore and Punjab. His two younger sons, Shehbaz Sharif and Abbas Sharif (died 2013), have also had successful political careers. Along with the Bhuttos, this dynasty has dominated Pakistani politics since the 1980s. The Sharifs do not appear to have relied on extensive marriage networks with other influential families as much as some other politically engaged lineage groups, but there is no doubt that there have been some strategically beneficial unions in the Sharif family (see figure 7.1).

The Sharifs demonstrate the effectiveness of solidarity within the lineage group. Nawaz and his brother Shahbaz maintained a coherent front throughout their political careers and arguably continue to do so. Nevertheless, they have benefited from the support of affinal connections. Nawaz's late wife, Begum Kulsoom, was a formidable politician in her own right. Like her husband, she came from a Kashmiri family and was the granddaughter, on her maternal side, of a famous wrestler known as The Great Gama.[1] It still rather baffles me how people know such trivia, but clearly it's important enough that people in rural Pakistan, at least, are aware of such connections to a variety of forms of greatness. Nawaz and Kulsoom Sharif's two daughters both married men with strategic connections. Maryam Sharif married a retired military officer, Captain Safdar, who is an elected politician in his own right. Captain Safdar introduces a slightly controversial element into the Sharif family network. As a vocal critic of secular politicians, he has often stood up for causes that Nawaz Sharif and his brother have largely avoided. Captain Safdar

Industrialist and Populist Challengers

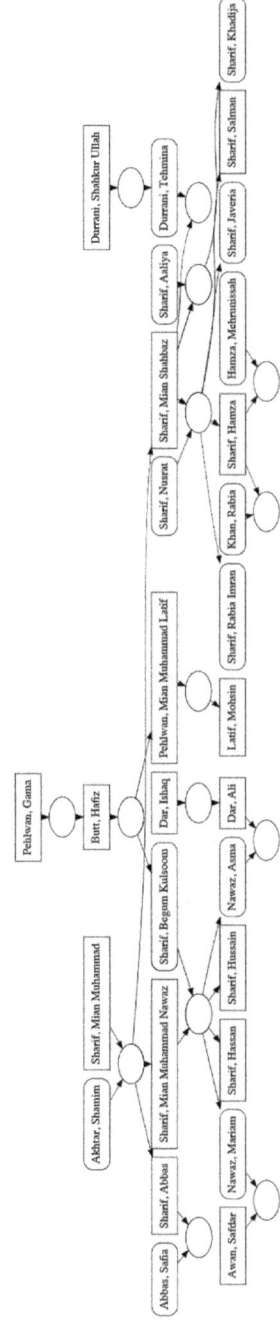

Figure 7.1 The Sharif Kinship Network. *Source*: Author generated graph.

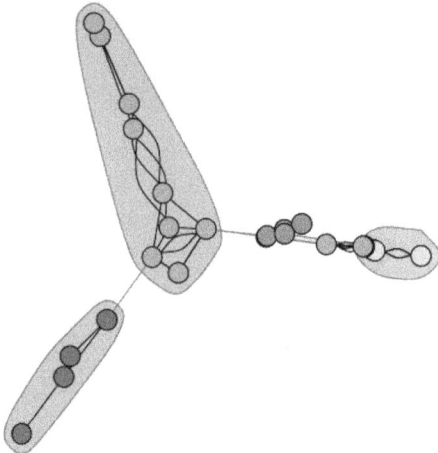

Figure 7.2 The Kinship Network of the Sharifs. The names have been removed to allow the clusters to stand out. Within each cluster, there is at least one prominent politician. *Source*: Author generated graph.

praised Mumtaz Qadri, the assassin of Salman Taseer, the former Governor of Punjab, for example. On another occasion, Nawaz Sharif had to suspend Captain Safdar's party membership of PML-N for openly insulting some key supporters from Khyber-Pukhtunkhwa province (Mahmood 2012)[2].

Nawaz Sharif's younger daughter, Asma, married the son of Ishaq Dar, a prominent Pakistani politician who served as a federal minister in Nawaz Sharif's government. Begum Kulsoom's brother's son, Mohsin Latif, was a member of the Punjab Provincial Assembly (PML-N) until 2015.

Shahbaz Sharif and his son Hamza both have two wives.[3] Shahbaz's first wife, Nusrat, is his first cousin. As with landlords, close marriages like this are crucial for consolidating resource control and have a higher likelihood of minimal disruption to the household. His second wife, Tehmina Durrani, is the daughter of, Shahkur Ullah Durrani, a former governor of the State Bank of Pakistan. Unlike his first marriage, the second union was not only outside his *biradari*, but also outside his *qaum*. The Durranis are a famous Pukhtun *qaum*.

In addition to any political advantage the Sharif's may enjoy as a result of their marriage network, there are also frequent reports of the net worth of the individual adult members of the Sharif family and their spouses (e.g., Khan and Ali 2014). It would appear that the super wealthy, regardless of *qaum, biradari,* or nationality, marry within comparable socioeconomic bands.

IMRAN KHAN AND *NAYA PAKISTAN*

In the summer of 2018, the outcome that was unthinkable a decade earlier happened. Imran Khan's Pakistan Tehrik-i-Insahf (PTI) party won a majority of seats in the National Assembly and formed a government. Like Zulfikar Bhutto, Imran Khan's personal charisma spearheaded a powerful coalition of disparate political agendas and ideologies that struck the right note at the right time. Imran Khan allied himself with individuals and groups who clearly shared few common interests, but they recognized that the time had come for a change of political elite. The Sharif family scandals had reached such a crescendo that both Nawaz and his daughter, Maryam, were sent to prison. The People's Party had not sufficiently recovered from the loss of Benazir and the disappointing performance of her widower, Asif Ali Zardari. Her son, Bilawal, although more seasoned and experienced than in either 2008 or 2013, remained underwhelming in many parts of Pakistan and the party wasn't able to mount an effective national campaign. The principle secular parties (or at least what passes for a secular party in Pakistan), the ANP and the MQM, had lost considerable ground to the wave of cult like following that had emerged around Imran Khan. In 2013, Imran Khan had galvanized the youth in a way that promised substantial gains in the future, *if* he and his PTI party didn't completely mess up in Khyber-Pukhtunkhwa (KP), which they had won for the first time. In 2018, for the first time in KP's history, the people returned the same party to a provincial majority. While this doesn't mean PTI made no mistakes at the provincial level, it is a strong indication that they got enough right to satisfy the majority of voters.

PTI's catchy slogan was *Naya Pakistan* or New Pakistan. Imran Khan promised to clean up the state and deal with the endemic corruption in some areas of government. He seemed to provide a way for Pakistan to claim pride in its accomplishments and move towards greater self-sufficiency. He spoke of the need to establish principles of equitable distribution in a country riven with some of the most extreme poverty on the planet alongside staggering wealth. Rather unnervingly, for some people, he also spoke articulately about the need to bring *all* Pakistanis along for brave new future—including groups with whom the Pakistan army had been effectively at war with for more than a decade. The Taliban are reported to have announced that Imran Khan had nothing to worry about from them in the 2013 election. One of the names people used to refer to him at the time was Taliban Khan. At the time, I remember conversations with secular minded Pakistanis who wanted to like Imran Khan because he seemed sincere and cosmopolitan, but found themselves decidedly uneasy about anyone that the Taliban might find acceptable.

Some of his allies in 2018 were as questionable as in 2013, but PTI nevertheless managed to ride a pluralist wave to victory.

One of the questions I am periodically asked about this *Naya Pakistan* "revolution" is whether this signals a diminishing power of kinship politics and the strength of party ideological agendas. Everything is possible, but I'm afraid I'm skeptical of anything that purports to be genuinely novel or new. Pakistan has had charismatic leaders in the past and clearly there is a pattern of renewal in the system in which space can open up for something that appears radically different from everything that came before. Z. A. Bhutto's PPP in the late 1960s was fresh and promised a profound departure from the ostensibly conservative[4] military regime of Ayub Khan and the preceding chaos of unstable governments before the declaration of martial law. The PPP certainly didn't succeed in effecting a genuine Islamic socialism, nor did they diminish the rising levels of corruption. And of course, it turned out to be a real boost for one of the more powerful and long-lived dynastic power networks in Pakistan's relatively short history. Time will tell if Imran Khan and PTI can introduce the types of systemic changes that might dislodge the patron-client networks that have maintained a consistent stranglehold on the Pakistan state and its preceding regimes. One thing we do know, with some certainty, however, is that Imran Khan is not an absolute ruler at liberty to introduce sweeping institutional change within a single parliament. His base, apart from the rather unsavory characters like the late Sami Ul Haq, assassinated in his own home in Rawalpindi only a few months after the formation of the PTI government, includes some seriously mature political networks that abandoned PML-N, PML-Q and PPP for what they imagined, correctly as it happens, was the winning "team." I certainly don't want to sound flippant or imply that the consequences of Pakistan's elections aren't incredibly serious for all of Pakistan, the region and the global political community, *but,* it's hard not to think of the musical chairs of leadership as something of a farce. While it's true that there are profound differences between the party manifestos of some mainstream parties in Pakistan, in practice, what we have seen is a tussle between an elite minority who make bizarre deals that are completely unrelated, and sometimes contradict, party manifesto pledges. My conversation with an honest landlord in the run up to the 2013 elections was fascinating and horrifying in equal measure. He was disarming in his candor in admitting that he knew little to nothing about the national agenda of the party he was then supporting, but wanted to know that the winner would support him in his land disputes against his patrilateral cousins. The thought that the fate of the entire country's political future was being determined by a string of utterly parochial and self-serving interests remains deeply troubling.

It would be nice to report that Imran Khan at the very least managed to personally escape the usual requisite family connections, but of course that

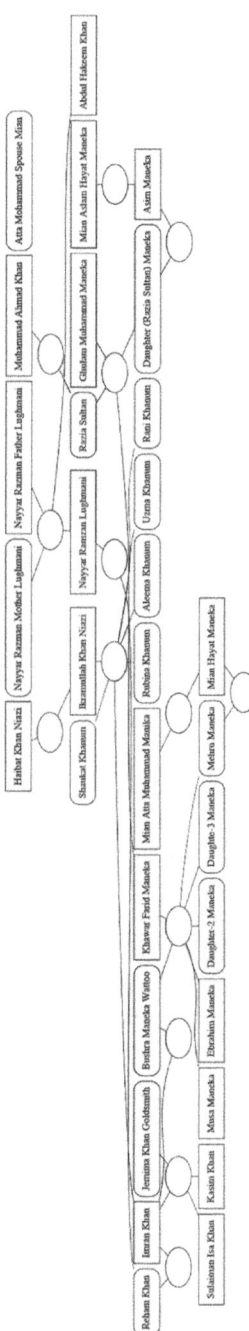

Figure 7.3 Imran Khan Kinship Network. *Source*: Author generated graph.

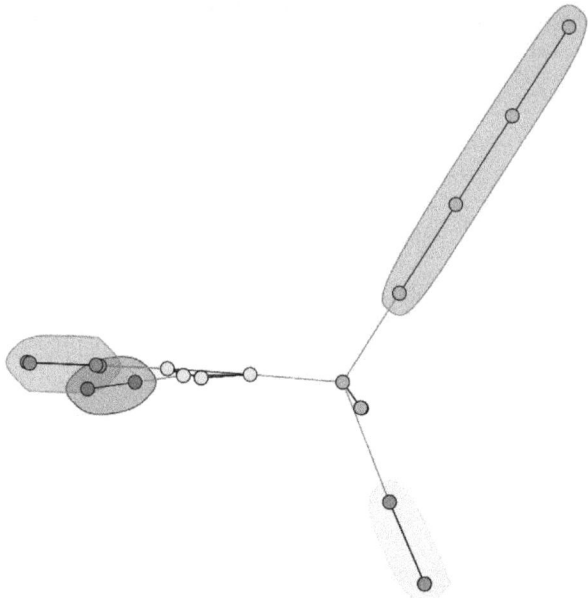

Figure 7.4 Imran Khan Kinship Network Showing Clusters of Related Families. The names have been removed to ease interpretation of the connections between clusters. *Note* that in each of these clusters, there is at least one active politician. *Source*: Author generated graph.

would be naïve and misleading. He did, perhaps, move Pakistan slightly closer to the pattern in the UK of class and elite school network being the dominant foundation for the political networking, but there's no escaping his personal family connections.

Imran Khan comes from a prominent political *biradari*. His family is from Mianwali, a Punjab District bordering KP. He is a member of the Niazi *qaum*, a well-respected, prominent political family that have not only held important political offices directly, but have played an important role behind the scenes in determining who can run and win in the elections. Imran's branch of the Mianwali Niazi family claim descent from Haibat Khan Niazi, a sixteenth-century general in Sher Shah Suri's army and was later made governor of Punjab.

So why he didn't win before if he was so well connected. There are a number of reasons for the "slow burn" of PTI and Imran Khan's political success. First, he didn't initially enter politics through his Niazi family political affiliations, though obviously he would have had the support of many family members. In the 1990s, PTI was effectively a one-man party. At that time, it was probably a party we might categorize as secular and progressive. He was clearly articulate and became something of a darling of western media. He knew how to say what would make sense to European and North American listeners. So long as he was an isolated voice in the wilderness, he could also afford to express what were probably his personal convictions. One of the strategies he adopted to grow PTI's support base was of course to curb some of his earlier progressive views. If we give him the benefit of the doubt and assume that this reflects a sincere transformation in his political thinking, then it's still possible to imagine that he expresses his personal convictions articulately and effectively. Tactically, his shift to a more religious political ground helped to neutralize potential criticism of his days as a cricket star based in England. His first wife, Jemima Khan née Goldsmith, while a substantial asset internationally and among cosmopolitan elite in the urban centers of Pakistan, was not necessarily appreciated by religious conservative politicians or their supporters. More importantly, the Goldsmiths have no Pakistani political party connections that might be called up on to deliver campaign support or votes.

Imran Khan shored up his areas of potential weakness in a number of ways. First, he is a skilled orator in both Urdu and English. From the earliest days of his entrance to politics, he has understood the need to control his own message. In interviews, he has demonstrated a mastery of keeping the conversation on his own terms. One of his most important talking points throughout his political career has been the need to address corruption in Pakistan. He has kept the focus on corruption like few others and can be given considerable credit for ensuring that the scandals revealed by the leaked Panama Papers didn't became "yesterday's" news but instead were continuously fed onto the front pages of Pakistan's newspapers and repeatedly rose as talking points in Pakistan's television and online media news. Immediately after the revelation of Nawaz Sharif's family financial assets, Imran Khan held a press conference on Pakistani television and demanded that the Pakistan government take these allegations as seriously as western democracies like Britain. He compared Nawaz Sharif's family investments with those of David Cameron's father. Cameron's father, he argued, had only a fraction of the investments that the Sharifs had, but the Parliament was investigating the legal implications of these and reviewing whether there were any potential conflicts of interest as a result. Cameron, he argued was being properly scrutinized and his political future hung in the balance. In contrast, Nawaz Sharif and his advocates asserted that there was no case to answer and the National Assembly was rolling over and accepting this without any serious challenge. Much to the PML-N's discomfort, the many millions invested through the law firm of Mossack Fonseca became a common talking point throughout the country regardless of class or political affiliation (Zaidi 2016). Even long-standing ordinary PML-N voters were unhappy with the revelations and were not completely persuaded by the family's explanations for the origin of the wealth.

To be sure, like all Pakistani politicians, Imran Khan has also been accused of financial and other impropriety as well. For many Pakistani politicians, this is their Achilles Heel. Regardless of how "clean" an individual politician may be in his or her personal transactions, there is some certainty that they will be allied to people with decidedly murkier records. In one of my first jobs, I worked in a sandwich shop run by a New Yorker who had relocated to Austin. He gave me a fantastic education in the realities of politics in a world enmeshed in corruption. At the time, I liked Mario Cuomo, then mayor of New York, and thought he should run for president. My boss, who was an old school Republican (by which I mean there was plenty of common ground between him and any mainstream Democrat), shook his head and said that would be impossible. "Why?" I asked somewhat defiantly. My boss said very confidently, "No one gets to be mayor of New York without making deals with the Mafia. Republican, Democrat, honest, corrupt it makes no difference. You simply cannot get elected without making some deals with the devil in a big city that has endemic organized crime." There is no equivalent organization like the Mafia in Pakistan, by which I mean there is no romanticized group around which myths of ambiguous nobility and honor have arisen that principally exists to carry out criminal activities. People use the term mafia in association with various criminal activities, notably the Land Mafia, but they are far from a nationally organized crime syndicate and to date, I know of no unifying rituals or symbolism associated with them. Instead, there are multiple power bases that control votes and resources in specific domains. The people involved are decidedly self-interested and operate within sometimes shockingly narrow horizons. In other words, they sometimes have surprisingly little ambition to control circumstances beyond their current "empires."

Amassing the necessary support to win any election, regardless of the level, demands alliances with different power networks. Imran Khan's victories have very evidently been the result of his and his closest allies' willingness to build bridges with people and organizations whose ideological positions may appear contradictory to their own. Some, perhaps many, of those people have unblemished histories in relation to financial corruption, but where there is great wealth, there will always be questions. Anyone coming from a landowning rural elite must contend with some awkward questions of how the land came to be owned by their ancestors in the first place. Sometimes, they can claim to be the first people in the area and so they claimed ownership without compromising other people's economic positions. That must surely be rather rare in a country like Pakistan that has been continuously populated for several thousand years. I know of at least one medium sized village in Rawalpindi Division in which the landowners have a narrative of continuous ownership that goes back more than 1000 years, but there is also a contrasting narrative that would suggest they were given the land by the British following the collapse of the Sikh kingdom. The truth is clearly not entirely revealed by either narrative. They might have been the original inhabitants whose land possession was compromised by the arrival of powerful Sikh families who dispossessed the locals. In which case, both narratives would be true. Working in areas populated by people who were largely illiterate until very recently, that were not "important" in grand political narratives, leaves one with a lack of documented historical evidence of what happened. This doesn't make the history any less significant or important for contemporary populations, but it does make it harder to reconstruct the competing descriptions of what actually happened. Industrialists can at least usually answer the question of how their families came to own the factories that provide their wealth. Unfortunately, such stories are not always as squeaky clean as people might like. Stories of takeovers and forced expulsions are common in relation to how individuals came to own specific properties.

Stories of corruption or theft are rampant across Pakistan, but like the opposing stories of nobility and hard work, mustn't be taken at face value. There is a factionalism that drives such stories. Supporters opt for exaggerated stories of virtue while opponents either invent or exaggerate dastardly characterizations of their enemies. I recall many occasions when people from the village I have worked in for the past two decades have told visitors about my virtues. I hardly recognize myself in those descriptions, but I am grateful that they defend my reputation.

Imran Khan certainly knew how to form strategic relationships through his charisma and persuasive charm. If that were sufficient, then his electoral success might have occurred considerably earlier. In the 1990s, he was, perhaps, limited by his first marriage. His marriage to the wealthy English socialite and activist, Jemima Goldsmith, while potentially a bridge building union with Europeans, did little tie him to important political families in Pakistan. The fact that her paternal grandfather was Jewish didn't help, but was largely an issue for those who didn't like Imran Khan for other reasons as well. The Jewish connection, however, distant or spurious, was fuel to those who wanted an overtly anti-Israeli, anti-Semitic agenda. Imran Khan probably isn't either anti-Israeli or anti-Semitic in ways that would satisfy hard liners in the Muslim world.

His second marriage, although short lived, was a more strategically useful alliance for PTI. The short lived union with Reham Khan, gave him a familial connection to a prominent political family in Khyber-Pukhtunkhwa. Her paternal uncle was Abdul Hakeem Khan, the former governor of Khyber-Pukhtunkhwa and Chief Justice of the Peshawar High Court. As a journalist, she may also have been instrumental in advising Imran Khan on his media presence, though to be fair, that is an area in which he probably needed no help.

Imran Khan's second marriage lasted only 9 months. It's hard to know what to make of such a short marriage, but it came at a strategic time as Imran Khan shored up his support among the military and broadened his reach into Punjab. The marriage has not proven entirely helpful for Imran Khan's public image, however. Despite the strategic advantage he may have gained from marrying into a well-connected family, the publication of Reham Khan's damning memoir has caused some embarrassment and triggered a host of denials from Imran Khan himself, as well as his allies and some of the people named in the book (Khan 2018).

His third marriage, to Bushra Maneka, provides an interesting example of complicated connectivity. The immediately obvious advantage of the marriage is that this gave Imran Khan the chance to consolidate his connections to Pakistan's sufi religious communities. Imran and Bushra met at Pakpattan, the site of one of the most important Chishti shrines in South Asia. Apparently, Imran's growing interest in sufism led him to the shrine of Baba Farid Shakar Ganj, a thirteenth-century South Asian saint, where he met the Maneka family. The Maneka family is politically influential in the area and Bushra was considered an accomplished sufi scholar. She became Imran's spiritual advisor, or *murshid*. She was married at the time they met to a man named Khawar Maneka. Khawar is the son of Ghulam Muhammad Maneka, a former minister in Benazir Bhutto's cabinet and the brother of Ahmad Raza Maneka, elected to the National Assembly in 2018 with Pakistan Muslim League (N). Bushra and Khawar had five children together. Their eldest daughter is married to the son of Mian Atta Mohammad Manika, former member of the Provincial Assembly in the Okara District, just near Pakpattan.

The religious landscape in Pakistan is fractured and contentious. Despite being one of only two countries created as a safe homeland for a religious community (the other being Israel), the tensions between Pakistan's religious groups has been a persistent feature within the country since independence. By marrying his Sufi spiritual advisor, Imran Khan signaled his commitment to Islam and to the more spiritual flavor of Islam represented by Sufism, as opposed to the more literal approach of Wahhabism. The political influence of the Manekas in the Pakpattan area has been historically significant and until Pervez Musharraf introduced the requirement to hold a Bachelor's degree for the National Assembly, Bushra Maneka's former father-in-law, Mian Ghulam Muhammad,[5] had been a successful and influential politician from the area. PTI already had secured the support of a number of Deoband groups, thanks to their strong support in Khyber-Pukhtunkhwa. Building bridges into the Barelvi dominated Punjab was instrumental to electoral success in 2018. It would be absurd to credit this support entirely to a simple marriage between two people, but as I have tried to argue throughout this book, there is no such thing as a "simple" marriage. Marriages are bridges within networks and they must not be assumed to be individualistic unions between individuals. They are the composite bridging of groups of people and as such, are not solely matters for two individuals. Imran Khan has defied a number of rules throughout his career, both as a world class cricketer and as a political activist and politician, but in the end, I think it's not a coincidence that his greatest electoral success came after two strategic marriages that allowed him to develop relations with political networks that appealed to groups he had hitherto not managed to attract to his particular bandwagon.

These relations matter, in part, because it made it possible for politicians across Pakistan to abandon their earlier political party affiliations and align themselves under a PTI umbrella. One good example of this re-alignment can be found in Attock District. One of the regionally powerful family networks I discussed in chapter six, headed by Major Tahir Sadiq, joined PTI for the 2018 elections. Major Tahir Sadiq has not dramatically altered his political agenda, so far as I can tell. Nor has he compromised his status or position in Attock District. His family continues to hold a number of elected positions and influence politics far beyond the boundaries of Attock or Pindi Division. They have, for the moment, thrown their support behind PTI, but it is clear from their history that their loyalty is contingent on the continued success of PTI. Like their close allies, the Choudhrys of Gujarat, they respect power and success. When General Musharraf was on the rise, the Choudhrys of Gujarat and the Khattars of Attock happily formed the backbone of PML-Q. When it was clear that the Q League had lost the ability to win elections, the Khattars formed an independent group, Major Tahir Sadiq Group, which could provide strategic support to the governing party on an issue by issue basis. Clearly, Imran Khan managed to persuade them that there was more to be gained by formally accepting the PTI label and they have done so. Such practices have a long tradition among landowners in Punjab. In the waning decades of the British Raj, the formation of the Unionist Party demonstrated the extent to which landowners were capable of manipulating or twisting either religious or civil law to impose and maintain the legitimacy of their landownership.

CONCLUSION: PARALLEL PATTERNS

The parallels between national-level political parties and landlords in rural Punjab is telling. It may seem obvious to people who pay attention to grassroots politics, but it is worth making explicit. Politics in Pakistan is messy and dangerous. Political parties do not replicate themselves without effort. There must be both robust mechanisms for maintaining some continuity over time as well as sufficient resilience to adapt and maneuver in response to abrupt shifts in the political landscape. Descent-based dynasties are an important element in the formula for successful reproduction, but they introduce the same brittleness that can compromise landlord families trying to fend off the near constant attempts to chip away at their land holdings and natural resources. Carefully balancing near and more distant marriages creates social connections outside the agnatic lineage. Such extra-agnatic bridging comes with a certain measure of risk because there isn't the same guaranteed shared household identity. Affinal groups can and do fall out. There is never total confidence in mutual support if the narrow interests of the groups are contradictory, however, in addition to the shared bond of marriage, the families discussed in both chapter 6 and 7 also share a clear class interest. Chaudhry Zahoor Elahi and his sons didn't select marriage partners at random. They arranged marriages with prominent families who benefited from a high degree of status quo protection who were not in Gujerat, their home District. Landlords frequently fall out, at least temporarily, over disputed claims to the same land, however, that is less likely when the affinal group is on the other side of the province or even in another province. Moreover, all of the families discussed have moved beyond a highly provincial focus on tracts of land and have entered into a competitive game of political influence that spans regions. The result is a class of elite power manipulators who *use* many of the techniques of landlords, but are considerably more detached from the foundational resource upon which their power may be built. They have entered into a sphere of political elite that shares much with the global financial elite who long ago lost track of the intrinsic value of actual things and instead manipulate the perceived value to underpin their own "score card" in the new Great Game of political influence.

The extent to which these partisan elites control the systems of power brokerage is highly constrained. Pakistan, unlike some countries in Middle East and North Africa, has resisted efforts to consolidate power into a small cabal. Just as kinship systems provide continuity and prevent strong state formation, so too do they prevent elite political families from eliminating their rivals. The path to power is through complex, hybrid alliances composed both of lineage mates and competitor lineages. The rhetorically preferred marriage of like-with-like is not a viable strategy on its own, but mixed with the right number of marriages between *different* households arranged at judicious times, households can both maintain and expand their influence. Miscalculations in these arrangements can trigger devastating consequences for households and their dependents. Is it any wonder, then, that Pakistanis who are in the "power" game, struggle to control their children's marriages? The relationships aren't isolated romantic partnerships between two star-struck, individual lovers. Rather, they are corporate agreements between households that all have a great deal to lose if things don't go as planned.

Before we judge Pakistani elites too harshly, we should remind ourselves that historically the majority of marriages in Britain and the United States occur between individuals who meet in education or work and so typically wind up being of comparable socioeconomic status. Marriage isn't as effective a bridge building tool between households in the northern Europe and North America, so it's hardly surprising that political families in those places worry more about comparability of socioeconomic status than actual political lineage, but the interconnections of class are there. In recent decades, many elite Pakistanis appear to have adopted a similar strategy of controlling their children's social environment, but leaving the actual choice of marriage partner up to them.

On a visit to a village in Rawalpindi Division, Punjab, I met with a very old, respected woman. She is said to be the oldest person in her village. We spoke at length about marriages and the importance of ensuring that one's children married "well." She told me that these days, it was right that young women should choose their own husband. I was stunned and asked for clarification about how that could happen. She told me that young women were able to get education now and even work if they wanted to. I didn't press her on the point, but I assumed that she meant that these were suitable opportunities for getting to know appropriate young men. I asked if her granddaughters could marry *anyone* they wanted and she laughed and assured me that they could—only they mustn't marry vulgar men. I turned to her son, who was sitting on the side of the room listening to the conversation and asked him if that were true, could his daughter choose her own marriage partner. He smiled and shrugged and said that his mother was very wise and if she said so, then it must be true. The granddaughters are far too young to get married so I am still waiting to see how those marriages actually happen, but the contrast with my first interviews on the topic in the late 1990s couldn't be more striking. In the late 1990s, I can't recall ever hearing a single person in the rural areas contemplating allowing their children, and certainly not their daughters, to take the lead in selecting their marriage partner. Today, it's not only imaginable, it appears to be happening.

NOTES

1. While I doubt that Nawaz Sharif's affinal connection to The Great Gama will have won him many votes, it may have helped raise some awareness of his presence in certain circles—so it certainly won't have hurt him.

2. The presence of a disruptive and potentially threatening close relative is a common phenomenon in landlord families (usually a younger brother), so while there is no evidence that Captain Safdar's contentious behaviors are in any way coordinated

by the Sharifs, the very fact that they have a close connection to someone who might be "unleashed" on occasion can be politically expedient in some circumstances.

3. The rumors of clandestine marriages have been denied by both men and their supporters. For the purposes of this book, the truth of such marriages is irrelevant, because the political benefit of secret marriages is considerably harder to discern.

4. Though it is worth noting that the categories of liberal and conservative don't lend themselves to easy equivalencies across national contexts. Ayub Khan was not particularly socially conservative, but his government was an ally of the United States in the Cold War and supported private investment and some degree of market liberalization. Rather bizarrely in my view, that can be called conservative in the United States.

5. His wife, Razia Sultan, had also come from a politically influential family before Partition. Her father was Ahmad Khan, former Chief Justice of the Bhopal High Court in India (*The News* 2018).

Conclusion

Systemic Resilience and Robustness

Systems theoretical approaches offer a number of advantages for understanding complex phenomena, but they also make the analyses more challenging. Simple systems don't pose so much of a problem, but typical real-life examples of human systems often do. To begin with, systems that guide and inform human behavior don't operate in isolation. So while we can logically delineate discrete systems of human culture, politics, economics, and society, in practice, these are neither discrete nor "complete" without reference to other systems. We might use the term "sub" to refer to constituent systems, but that suggests that there is an overarching logic that regulates them all and that does not appear to be the case empirically. Instead, we find competing systems that can be based on contradictory relationships.

Leaf's (2007) thoughtful discussion of empirical formalism in the natural and social sciences makes an important distinction between the use of mathematical formalism to *describe* a system, a very useful technique in the natural sciences, and the fact that in the social sciences, the data themselves are the formal systems. The challenge, according to Leaf, is to identify and represent these systems, in ways that do not introduce, or contaminate to use his word, the culturally indigenous system with spurious foreign systems. The classic example of this is Rivers' genealogical method. Rivers employed a formal system to generate useful genealogical data about individuals, but neglected to adequately account for the system that formed the foundation of kinship among people in the Torres Straits.

The logic of descent reckoning, for example, is coherent and informationally economical. It allows individuals to situate themselves with a kinship position in relation to others in their kin group. Unilineal systems provide a simple mechanism for truncating some of the complexity of descent to focus on the "lines" that are deemed to be important within the cultural context. This can be harnessed to organize the distribution of labor and other resources as well as make difficult forms of cooperation more feasible. Unilineal systems rather quickly encounter limitations when the demand for resources outstrips what is available within a descent group, however, so these can be coupled with systems of alliance building, including but not exclusive to marriage.

The presence of kinship as a *system* has been present throughout this book, however much it may have appeared that individuals were manipulating, bending or even breaking the rules of the system. The constraining logic of kinship underpins cooperation and competition, including those that turn violent, even when it appears that people are taking idiosyncratic strategic, bespoke decisions and actions. The fact that one of the most violent insurgencies in Pakistan's history must invest consistently and heavily into breaking down the kinship connections of their recruits is a telling, if depressing, testament to the influence that kinship has on individuals.

CHECKING POWER

Kinship is complex and multifaceted. It has functional and symbolic effects on society and these defy simplistic moral judgement. Although there are caveats, one of the impacts on Pakistan has been to prevent the development of unchecked power. Clearly, it has not prevented mass accumulation of wealth by a minority, nor has it prevented state resources from being dominated and controlled by family groups for their own and their allies benefit. The disparity in access to resources between the wealthiest and poorest Pakistanis is shocking and the evidence would suggest that the poorest 20% have remained roughly where they were while the wealthiest minority have enjoyed a dramatic increase in wealth (Jaffrelot 2015). So how can I possibly argue that kinship has served as a check on the accumulation of power? Like Barth's (1981) response to Asad's (1972) sensible and coherent criticism, I focus not on the end result of a system of inequality, but rather on the mechanisms by which those inequalities were created. Asad rightly argued that despite the game playing that Barth described so eloquently, there were clearly class barriers to who was *able* to participate. A more Marxist oriented analysis would, Asad argued, shed light on the forces of production that reproduced the class asymmetries that marked Swat society. Barth acknowledged that there were indeed class barriers, but argued that they didn't exist *a priori* from the people in the society. They were the product of individual transactions carried out by individuals. Martin's (2016) cogent critique of landlord classes in Punjab is not wrong—they do indeed siphon off any surplus they can access and they use their position to try and consolidate and accumulate greater wealth and power. They have not, to date, managed to consolidate power into a tightly controlled, cooperative central collection of people. What we find are competing groups at every level. No level of the hierarchy is unified or corporate in the sense that they are able to pool resources and influence to bring about a radical shift in power in their exclusive favor. This book has been an examination not of the inequality *per se*, but rather the adaptive properties of a system that does not eradicate inequality.

I started by suggesting that the history of invading elite "others" has resulted in a complex pluralist political landscape in which the rulers and the ruled were separated from one another. Those in power claimed some type of distinction from those over whom they ruled. The Hindu *varna* system builds in logical barriers between the rulers (both spiritual and temporal) and the masses over whom they had some authority. The arrival of Muslim elites, then Sikh elites, continued the tradition of the rulers *not* being *of* the people, but rather a special category apart. Britain's roughly two centuries of control exacerbated this difference even more, but introducing not only an elite who were distinct, but an elite who rotated in and out of the country and parasitically drained the country of its surplus production to the benefit of the metropole. Such a benefit should not be inferred to suggest that there wasn't exploitation occurring in Britain. Wallerstein makes clear in his historical assessment of the rise of capitalism and imperialism, that while it is possible to identify core and periphery regions within capitalism, exploitation occurs throughout the system (Wallerstein 1974).

The effect of what I've called waves of elites who were symbolically and economically separated from the people over whom they had some measure of control was to encourage a sophisticated conceptual ability to maintain cognitively contradictory ideas simultaneously. In part, this is what makes the Pakistani political landscape *adaptive*. It has built in mechanisms for individuals to maneuver, when necessary, in ways that don't fundamentally challenge or threaten key features of the system. One can, for example, support and be loyal to, structures of power that run counter to one's *own* self-interest. One can be "friends" with one's "enemies" (and vice versa). Factional borders can and do shift and allegiance is never irrevocable.

Descent and alliance in kinship systems provide both robustness *and* resilience—two attributes that any system requires to successfully reproduce over time. The pull between allowing one or the other primacy in historical anthropological debates distracts from the extent to which neither is sustainable without the other. Consolidation of resources and power benefits from emphasizing descent bonds, while expansion of influence and insurance against catastrophic failure depends on alliance ties. In Pakistan, rhetorically both are highly valued and the site of a great deal of contestation.

MATERIAL CONSEQUENCES OF KINSHIP

Kinship wouldn't be particularly interesting if it didn't have a genuine impact in the world. After taking you through what might have seemed an esoteric meander through the anthropological garden of kinship, I showed how kinship, in the forms of lineage (*biradari*), family, and household, both generate and manage serious conflict at the local level. Land disputes, always contentious even among groups that do not claim ownership of the land itself, but instead only claim usage rights, are particularly challenging in rural Pakistan today. The rise in the value of land, population growth, environmental changes that have made water more scarce and soil quality progressively harder to maintain, have come face to face with a volatile political arena in which no part of the country has been spared. Land disputes have become more violent and more hotly contested as a result. The mechanisms for managing land disputes are, as they have always been, opportunistic and contingent on available resources, both human and material, but they only make sense in contexts in which kinship is present. I tried to show the ways in which kinship is at the heart of serious disputes—both their causes and their resolutions.

Venturing a bit outside the traditional comfort zone of a cultural anthropologist, I applied the principles of using marriage and descent networks to make sense of some of Pakistan's most successful elected politicians. Starting with a regionally powerful political network based in the north west of Punjab, I show how strategic marital connections have contributed much needed national level credibility to a relatively less powerful provincial kingpin. Provincial or not, however, it is thanks to such regional connectedness that another potentially regionally constrained political network managed to become major players at the national level. The game of musical chairs that has gone on between factions of the PML and the PPP over the past five decades was ostensibly broken in 2018 by the success of a party formed in the 1990s and led by a charismatic celebrity. Despite the initial possibility that this represented a fresh change, however, it is possible that much of the success for the new party has actually come from former supporters of the two major parties of government (PPP and PML factions) jumping ship and joining forces with the successful PTI. While I would not want to deny the importance of ideology or party manifestos in their entirety, I note with some caution that the success of PTI may also be built upon the strength of both descent and recent marital network bonds.

BEYOND REGIONAL AND ELECTORAL POLITICS

One area that fell beyond the scope of this book was an examination of kinship in the context of rising radicalization and the use of political violence. Again, this falls typically outside the usual domains of expertise of cultural anthropologists (with some exceptions) and I take seriously Werbner's (2010) concerns about attempting to contort anthropological expertise to comment on domains that do not lend themselves, easily, to the kinds of methods we normally rely on. My direct experience of insurgents and their communities is very slim, so I am not in a position to offer an ethnographically grounded analysis of ideas of security and the ways in which the state has sought to control citizens. Nevertheless, I have argued throughout this book that the bedrock of kinship has served to reinforce entrenched power relations in the country through the political fluidity and instability created by a succession of weak states. This has a number of consequences, including the production and reproduction of the mechanisms for providing continuity and predictability which, in turn, have undermined the development of strong state institutions that might enable vibrant and productive forms of civil society. As a result, civil society has, for better or worse, been dominated by kinship throughout much of Pakistan's history. The inadequacy of this arrangement for addressing social aspirations has been clear for decades, but came to a head with the collapse of Afghanistan and the spread of revolutionary ideologies that preached a Manichaean version of Islam in which simplistic tropes of good and evil become manifest in global and regional politics. Implementing a "pure" Islam and Islamic law has, at times, meant challenging traditional kinship obligations and responsibilities. There has been a wave of proselytizing Islamic leaders promising greater social fairness and equity and an end to the stranglehold of political elite families over the country. This attack on lineages as corporate units has sown considerable change in the country. The obvious violence that has come with these changes grabs the headlines, but it is important not to allow the violence to become the only story. In chapter 4, I examined the role of kinship as both a cause of conflict as well as one of the principle vehicles for managing and resolving conflict in local contexts. I suggested in that chapter that the landlords in Punjab and the peasants in Khyber-Pukhtunkhwa, the Federally Administered Tribal Areas and in north India all existed in cultural and social environments in which conflicts were systemically meaningful and regulated. The sociocultural construction of conflict is a specific historical product of the interaction of values, economic interests and social relations. I hinted that the sustainability of the communities was closely tied to their ability to flexibly adapt to differing levels of conflict. All of the ethnographies I referred to in that chapter shared an important message about the normativity of conflict. In other words, while the conflict may appear frightening and traumatizing to visitors from other cultures, they fall within the bounds of what are deemed normal disputes within those contexts. They are not traumatic to local people. Locals are able to give meaning to the arguments and the fights and continue with their ordinary lives unaffected. This is not to say that people on the ground don't care about these conflicts or that they don't get upset, but only that this does not lead to a collapse of other critical social or cognitive functions.

Moving beyond regional conflicts and the violence associated with elections, there has undoubtedly been a rise in politically motivated violence across Pakistan and the wider region. This increase began before 9/11, but has taken a dramatic turn for the worse following the invasions of Afghanistan and Iraq. Violence across the country has been on the increase since the Soviet invasion of Afghanistan in 1979 and especially since their withdrawal. The availability of weapons, always relatively widespread in certain parts of the country, has spread dramatically across all parts of the country. The presence of private security has spread and is increasingly armed. In the early 1980s, when I first lived in Pakistan, most wealthy households had a *chowkidar* (guard), but they were normally only armed with a large staff. If they had guns, they kept them out of sight. Purchasing a weapon to carry out a feuding act was not a casual thing and involved either dependence on a wealthy patron or several months of saving one's surplus resources.[1] The Soviet withdrawal from Afghanistan in 1989 left a vacuum of power that led to an explosion of local arms manufacturers as well as a vibrant trade in Chinese made small arms sales. The first time I went to Peshawar, I went to a market where I could have bought a bazooka,[2] but Peshawar and that market, stood out as exceptional at the time. In recent decades, such a purchase would be possible in a host of other markets and cities around the country—though I expect these days if I were to show the interest I showed back in 1982, I would certainly arouse well justified suspicion and would be reported to the intelligence services.

Pakistan has undergone profound social changes that are connected to the political violence it has endured. One manifestation of those social changes is a diminishment in the overt authority of the family over the individual. Individual rights are now more acknowledged and valorized. Individuals are charged with making key decisions and increasingly, that includes the selection of one's marriage partner. It also seems to be polarizing society in ways that reflect similar phenomena in Europe and the United States. The so-called progressives have taken a more militant position vis-a-vis individual rights and the importance of universal human rights, while the so-called conservatives have retreated into a more entrenched and intolerant position regarding sexuality and the importance of collective regulation of individual household members.[3] Consequently, while it's obvious that kinship has been under some strain and appears to have adapted in some possibly important ways, the importance of family, household and kinship ideologies should not be dismissed or under estimated. Many families have adopted a rhetoric of individual choice that resonates well with Western audiences, but like Westerners, they retain control over the key choices made by their members through controlling education and employment settings. Moreover, kinship continues to be a critical driver of security in the context of what may usefully be described as a scaled-up version of the traditional blood feuding societies described by ethnographers of Pakistan's tribal belts. Critically, there is evidence that isolating people from others is a significant factor in increasing extreme pro-group behavior required for some of the tactics adopted by insurgents (Pretus et al. 2018). Kinship is therefore not a "cure" to prevent radicalization, but insurgent groups *do* appear to understand the need to weaken and undermine people's connections to their families as part of their recruitment and training programs.

The crux of the situation today would seem to be rooted in a tension between the state exerting ever greater control over the individual, which risks undermining the authority and centrality of family and household, which, in turn, may facilitate more effective recruitment to radical ideological organizations unless there is a parallel initiative to enhance adherence and loyalty to the wider nation of Pakistan. Thus far, efforts to fast track strong feelings of national identity have been naïvely attempted through the establishment of a common enemy—India. That this has principally served to create a fragile reverence for the military, as the representative *par excellence* of the Pakistani nation, is hardly surprising.

CONCLUSION

The intellectual landscape of Pakistan studies is not entirely pessimistic. There are those who have marveled at the strengths of Pakistan and have suggested that some of the doom and gloom scenarios over emphasize some of the apparent weaknesses in Pakistan's national identify. If we understand national identity itself as akin to a Barthian symbolic marker of ethnicity (Barth 1969), that is not, in and of itself meaningful, but rather only operates to differentiate one group from another, then the ambiguity and contradictions of Pakistani nationalism are not necessarily unlike nationalisms that are deemed to be more stable and solid. Hamid (2011) paints a rather optimistic picture of Pakistan's potential future and argues that not only is nationalism over rated as a unifying force underpinning states, but that everywhere nationalism is contested and serves both to divide as well as unite. Although Hamid is a novelist rather than a social scientist, his observations on the tenuous nature of any national identity are well made. Hamid points to the wealth being generated in the country and like many left of center intellectuals, argues that if the Pakistan state could establish a fair tax base across all of its income earning residents, then it would have more than enough resource to deliver all of the public services that would support the middle classes and provide for greater social mobility among the poorest population groups. As of 2011, Hamid says that only 10% of Pakistan's Gross Domestic Product (GDP) was generated from taxation (Hamid 2011, 42). In contrast, Sri Lanka's tax contribution to GDP was 15%, India's 17%, Turkey's 24%, United States 28%, and Sweden 50%. With relatively modest increases in taxation, the Pakistan state could end its dependence on US aid and, according to Hamid, begin to assume control for its own destiny. It is a bit unfair, and a somewhat unkind, to criticize Hamid's optimism but there are a number of substantial obstacles to the stabilization and strengthening of public services delivery that are unrelated to state resource generation schemes. Some of those are simultaneously sources of stability and strength for the nation of Pakistan, or perhaps more accurately, for the *nations* of Pakistan. For while I agree with Hamid that nationalism is overrated as a *raison d'etre* for any state and there are clear examples of states that function effectively in the absence of agreement on the national identity and character, there are nevertheless clear bonds of loyalty among Pakistani and Pakistani Diaspora populations that work at cross purposes to the goals of the Pakistan state. In any event, while there are indisputable challenges to the nationalism as a unifying political philosophy for Pakistan *à la* Gellner (1983), the *idea* of unifying nations *within* Pakistan around ethnic or religious cleavages may serve both to prevent the formation of a genuine Pakistan nationalism while simultaneously offering important systems of congruence for the occasionally cooperating "national" units that make up Pakistan.

In the absence of Westphalian-style national unity, one of the questions any student of Pakistan must address is what binds the country together. Jinnah's famous slogan of unity in diversity makes a nice marketing strapline but it falls short of providing a satisfying explanation for the country's coherence. Dhulipala (2010) illustrates the fragility of attempts to establish a religious nation based on Islam, so religious unity was, and remains, an illusory aspiration rather than a genuinely uniting force. Here I have argued that chief among the systems of loyalty and reciprocity that furnish Pakistan its robust system of interconnectivity is kinship. This is not an idealized kinship or family as one might understand it in Britain or the United States, though it clearly has similarities with how kinship has operated at various times in the history of both of these areas. We need to think about Pakistani kinship as more like aristocratic politicking than a Norman Rockwell painting of ideal family harmony. The network construction and manipulation of Medieval Italian merchant families, perhaps most notoriously evidenced by the success of the Medici family offers a telling, if somewhat romanticized, illustration of the power of kinship as the basis for effective political networking (see Padgett and Ansell 2008 for a good analysis of the role of bridging network connections for consolidating political influence). The delicate politics of kinship in Pakistan is both affective and strategic. It serves to bind people in ways that offer robust stability and remarkable resilience in the face of shocks and crises. Kinship is not the only force that generates bonds of loyalty and reciprocity, of course, but it's one that blends well with a number of other patron-client exchange relationship systems.

Ultimately, while it is clear that the politics of Pakistan are turbulent and exhibit considerable complexity, there are important cultural patterns that are observable and knowable. These patterns are the result of relatively uncomplicated systems of relationship that have remarkably flexible adaptive properties that are productive and responsive to the considerable shocks that can arise from both internal and external forces. Kinship, coupled with ideas of patronage and clientalism, provide the foundational idea systems underpinning social organization at all levels of society, from the village all the way to the highest offices of state.

Tariq Ali (1983) posed an entirely legitimate question about the survivability of Pakistan. That question could be asked today and just as in 1983, sound arguments might be made for many potential outcomes. Pakistan has somehow managed to endure despite conditions that have led to state failure in other countries. Mughal and I (2016) argued that Pakistan should not be categorized as a "failed" state. We pointed to the ongoing functioning of a civil service that continued despite a landscape of periodically intense political volatility. Similarly, while Pakistan's military has interfered repeatedly with elected governments, this has not resulted in civil war. When citizens across the Arab world rose up in protest against autocratic regimes, a common sarcastic response as to why there was no Pakistan "Spring" was that Pakistan was a democracy. When I heard people say this it was always met with laughter. Apparently few, if any, people *believed,* that Pakistan's democracy was entirely legitimate or fair. They did not seem to believe that it represented their interests or the long-term interests of the country. They seem to have accepted that the representatives of the state were imperfect, venal, and self-serving. F. G. Bailey's (1963) classic ethnography of voters in Odisha (Orissa), India suggests this may be a widespread adaptive cultural pattern. While it is true that the voters believed that politicians in Odisha were not going to fulfill their campaign promises, they also knew that it was important to continue to give them a chance to do so. They never satisfied *all* promises, but they sometimes managed to achieve *some.* Evidently, this has not been good enough for many in either India or Pakistan, because there are armed insurgencies in both countries demanding more equitable resource redistribution. Nevertheless, the *majority* of people in Pakistan do not appear prepared to support armed revolution or open civil war. As I write this, I am conscious of an event I attended shortly before the Syrian uprising, at which most of the people who really knew Syria well were highly skeptical that the uprisings happening across the Arab world could happen in Syria. They were aware that some people were dissatisfied, but thought that there were enough social ties holding the distinct segments of society together to minimize the potential for revolutionary organization. Had the leadership of Syria not reacted the way they did, and had the tragic fallout from the invasion of Iraq not played out in the way it did, perhaps events in Syria would have gone very differently. Social capital in Pakistan is not infallible and requires constant maintenance and renewal. Kinship provides critical mechanisms for producing both the strong links that allow for the reproduction of coherent self-interest groups *and* the weak(er) links that ensure that there are clear relationships *between* those self-interest groups. These strong and weak ties are a crucial ingredient for the production of the social capital that enables Pakistan's civil society. Combining these strong and weak links ultimately allows Pakistanis to both reproduce their social relationships *and* build in resilience to adapt to extreme instability and change. Rather than seeing the strategic use of marriage and the highly orchestrated manipulation of kinship in the public sphere as a form of corruption, these should be understood as rational responses to extraordinary political and economic conditions.

NOTES

1. See Keiser's (1991) description of one of his principle informants and friends who had to save his money for 3 months in order to purchase a rifle to carry out a revenge killing.
2. In theory anyway. I'm not sure the market seller would really have been willing to sell such a lethal weapon to an inexperienced teenager who clearly didn't know what to do with such technology.
3. I use the terms progressive and conservative advisedly here. While there are overlaps with American notions of progressive and conservative, the areas in which they diverge can be jarring.

References

Ahmed, Akbar S. 1976. *Millenium and Charisma Among Pathans: A Critical Essay in Social Anthropology*. London: Routledge & Kegan Paul.

Ahmed, Akbar S. 1980. *Pukhtun Economy and Society: Traditional Structure and Economic Development in a Tribal Society*. London: Routledge.

Akhtar, Aasim Sajjad. 2019. "The Overdeveloped Alavian Legacy." In *New Perspectives on Pakistan's Political Economy: State, Class and Social Change*, edited by Matthew McCartney and S. Akbar Zaidi, 55–74. Cambridge: Cambridge University Press.

Alavi, Hamza. 1972. "The State in Post-Colonial Societies: Pakistan and Bangladesh." *New Left Review* 74 (July–August): 59–81.

Alavi, Hamza. 1983. "Class and State." In *Pakistan: The Roots of Dictatorship – the Political Economy of a Praetorian State*, edited by Hassan Gardezi and Jamil Rashid, 40–93. London: Zed Press.

Ali, Sameen Andaleeb Mohsin. 2018. "Staffing the State: The Politicisation of Bureaucratic Appointments in Pakistan." SOAS University of London. http://eprints.soas.ac.uk/26180.

Ali, Tariq. 1983. *Can Pakistan Survive?: The Death of a State*. Penguin.

Arghynbaev, Kh (Khalel). 1984. "Kinship System And Customs Connected With The Ban On Pronouncing The Personal Names Of Elder Relatives Among The Kazakhs." *Kinship And Marriage In The Soviet Union: Field Studies*, 40–59. http://ehrafworldcultures.yale.edu/document?id=rq02-009.

Armytage, Rosita. 2015. "The Social Lives of the Elite: Friendship and Power in Pakistan." *Asia Pacific Journal of Anthropology* 16 (5): 448–63. https://doi.org/10.1080/14442213.2015.1076887.

Armytage, Rosita. 2016. "Alliance of State and Ruling Classes in Contemporary Pakistan." *Economic & Political Weekly* 51 (31).

Asad, Talal. 1972. "Market Model, Class Structure and Consent: A Reconsideration of Swat Political Organisation." *Man* 7 (1): 74–94. https://doi.org/10.2307/2799857.

Bailey, F. G. 1963. *Politics and Social Change: Orissa in 1959*. Berkeley: University of California Press.

Balabanlilar, Lisa. 2012. *Imperial Identity in the Mughal Empire: Memory and Dynastic Politics in Early Modern South and Central Asia*. Paperback. London; New York: I.B. Tauris.

Barnes, J. A. 1969. "Graph Theory and Social Networks: A Technical Comment on Connectedness and Connectivity." *Sociology* 3 (2): 215–32. https://doi.org/10.1177/003803856900300205.

Barth, Fredrik. 1959a. *Political Leadership among Swat Pathans*. London: University of London, Athlone Press.

Barth, Fredrik. 1959b. "Segmentary Opposition and the Theory of Games: A Study of Pathan Organization." *The Journal of the Royal Anthropological Institute of Great Britain and Ireland* 89 (1): 5–21. https://doi.org/10.2307/2844433.

Barth, Fredrik. 1969. *Ethnic Groups and Boundaries: The Social Organization of Culture Difference*. Bergen; London: Universitetsforlaget; Allen & Unwin.

Barth, Fredrik. 1981. *Features of Person and Society in Swat: Collected Essays on Pathans*. London; Boston: Routledge & K. Paul.

Berlin, Brent, and Paul Kay. 1999. *Basic Color Terms: Their Universality and Evolution*. Stanford: CSLI Publications.

Bernard, H. Russell, and NetLibrary Inc. 2006. *Research Methods in Anthropology Qualitative and Quantitative Approaches*. Lanham: AltaMira Press.

Black-Michaud, Jacob. 1980. *Feuding Societies*. Oxford: Basil Blackwell.

Bohannan, Laura. 1958. "Political Aspects of Tiv Social Organization." In *Tribes without Rulers: Studies in African Segmentary Systems*, edited by John Middleton and David Tait, 33–66. London: Routledge and Kegan Paul.

Bohannan, Paul. 1957. *Justice and Judgement Amont the Tiv*. London: Oxford University Press.

Bott, Elizabeth. 1957. *Family and Social Network*. London: Tavistock.

Bouglé, Célestin. 1971. *Essays on the Caste System*. Translated by David F. Pocock. London: Cambridge University Press.

Buchler, Ira R., and Henry A. Selby. 1968. *Kinship and Social Organization: An Introduction to Theory and Method*. New York: The MacMillon Company.

Butt, Waseem Ashraf. 2016. "PML-Q Fields Shujaat's Sister for District Council Head." *Dawn*, January 18, 2016. www.dawn.com/news/1233720.

Carsten, Janet. 1997. *The Heat of the Hearth: The Process of Kinship in a Malay Fishing Community*. Oxford; New York: Clarendon Press; Oxford University Press.

Chaudhary, M. Azam. 1999. *Justice in Practice: Legal Ethnography of a Pakistani Punjabi Village*. Karachi: Oxford University Press.

Cheema, Ali, Hassan Javid, and Muhammad Farooq Naseer. 2013. "The Paradox of Dynastic Politics: Facts and Myths about the Political Dynasties in Punjab and Their Implications." *The Herald*, no. Special Election Issue: 11–15.

Comaroff, John L., and Simon Roberts. 1981. *Rules and Processes*. Chicago: University of Chicago Press.

Darwin, Charles. 2011. *On the Origin of Species by Means of Natural Selection, or the Preservation of Favoured Races in the Struggle for Life*. Empire Books.

Devji, Faisal. 2013. *Muslim Zion: Pakistan as a Political Idea*. London: C. Hurst & Co.

Dheer, Sanjay Bhola. 2016. *Mughal Emperors in India*. New Delhi: Mittal Book Agency.
Dhulipala, Venkat. 2010. "Rallying the Qaum: The Muslim League in the United Provinces, 1937–1939." *Modern Asian Studies* 44 (3): 603–40. https://doi.org/10.1017/S0026749X09004016.
Donnan, Hastings. 1988. *Marriage Among Muslims: Preference and Choice in Northern Pakistan*. Delhi: Hindustan Publishing Corporation.
Duindam, Jeroen. 2016. *Dynasties: A Global History of Power, 1300–1800*. Cambridge: Cambridge University Pres.
Dumont, Louis. 1970. *Homo Hierarchicus: The Caste System and Its Implications*. London: Weidenfeld & Nicolson.
Eglar, Zekiye. 1960. *A Punjabi Village in Pakistan*. New York: Columbia University Press.
Ernest, Gellner. 1983. *Nations and Nationalism: New Perspectives on the Past*. Ithaca: Cornell University Press.
Evans-Pritchard, E. E. 1937. *Witchcraft, Oracles and Magic Among the Azande*. Oxford: Oxford University Press.
Evans-Pritchard, E. E. 1940. *The Nuer: A Description of the Modes of Livelihood and Political Institutions of a Nilotic People*. Oxford: Clarendon Press.
Evans-Pritchard, E. E. 1976. *Witchcraft, Oracles and Magic among the Azande*. Abridged. Oxford: Oxford University Press.
Fateh, Tarek. 2010. *The Jew Is Not My Enemy: Unveiling The Myths That Fuel Muslim Anti-Semitism*. Toronto: McClelland & Stewart.
Fischer, Michael D., and Anthony Finkelstein. 1991. "Social Knowledge Representation: A Case Study." In *Using Computers in Qualitative Research*, edited by Nigel Fielding and Raymond Lee. 119–135. London: SAGE Publications.
Fischer, Michael D., and Dwight Read. 2005. *Kinship Algebra Expert System: A Computer Program and Documentation for Formal Modelling of Kinship Terminologies and the Simulation of Populations That under These Models*. Canterbury: CSAC Monographs. http://kaes.anthrosciences.net.
Fischer, Michael D., Dwight Read, and Stephen M. Lyon. 2005. "Introduction." *Cybernetics and Systems* 36 (8): 719–34. http://www.tandfonline.com/doi/abs/10.1080/01969720500356654.
Fischer, Michael D., Stephen M. Lyon, Daniel Sosna, and David Henig. 2013. "Harmonizing Diversity: Tuning Anthropological Research to Complexity." *Social Science Computer Review* 31 (1). https://doi.org/10.1177/0894439312455311.
Fortes, Meyer. 1949. *The Web of Kinship among the Tallensi*. London: Oxford University Press.
Foster, George M. 1965. "Peasant Society and the Image of Limited Good." *American Anthropologist* 67 (2): 293–315. http://www.jstor.org/stable/668247.
Foucault, Michel. 1977. *Discipline and Punish: The Birth of the Prison*. London: Allen Lane.
Foucault, Michel. 1978. *The History of Sexuality: An Introduction: 001*. New York: Pantheon Books.
Foucault, Michel. 2008. *The Birth of Biopolitics: Lectures at the Collège de France, 1978–79*. Edited by Michel Senellart and Collège de France. Michel Foucault: Lectures at the Collège de France. Basingstoke, England.

Fox, Richard G. 1969. *From Zamindar to Ballot Box: Community Change in a North Indian Market Town*. Ithaca: Cornell University Press.

Frembgen, Jürgen Waseem. 2014. *The Closed Valley: With Fiere Friends in the Pakistani Himalyas*. Karachi: Oxford University Press.

Gilmartin, David. 1988. "Customary Law and Shari'at in British Punjab." In *Shari'at and Ambiguity in South Asian Islam*, edited by Katherine P. Ewing, 43–62. Berkeley: University of California Press.

Gluckman, Max. 1955. *Custom and Conflict in Africa*. Oxford: Basil Blackwell.

Gluckman, Max. 1963. "Civil War and Theories of Power in Barotseland: African and Medieval Analogies." *The Yale Law Journal* 72 (8): 1515–46. https://doi.org/10.2307/794523.

Gluckman, Max. 1965. *The Ideas in Barotse Jurisprudence*. New Haven; London: Yale University Press.

Gluckman, Max, J. C. Mitchell, and J. A. Barnes. 1949. "The Village Headman in British Central Africa." *Africa: Journal of the International African Institute* 19 (2): 89–106. https://doi.org/10.2307/1156514.

Gomart, Emilie, and Antoine Hennion. 1999. "A Sociology of Attachment: Music Amateurs, Drug Users." Edited by John Law and J. Hassard. *The Sociological Review* 47 (1_suppl): 220–47. https://doi.org/10.1111/j.1467-954X.1999.tb03490.x.

Goodenough, Ward. 1965. "Yankee Kinship Terminology: A Problem in Componential Analysis." *American Anthropologist* 67 (5): 259–87.

Granovetter, Mark S. 1973. "The Strength of Weak Ties." Edited by Thomas S. Huang, Anton Nijholt, Maja Pantic, and Alex Pentland. *American Journal of Sociology*, Lecture Notes in Computer Science, 78 (6): 1360–80. https://doi.org/10.1086/225469.

Grima, Benedicte. 1992. *The Performance of Emotion among Paxtun Women*. Austin: University of Texas Press.

Guindi, Fadwa El, and Wesam al-Othman. 2013. "Transformationality and Dynamicality of Kinship Structure." *Structure and Dynamics: EJournal of Anthropological and Related Sciences* 6 (1). http://escholarship.org/uc/item/98z0r296.

Hamberger, Klaus, Michael Houseman, and Douglas R. White. n.d. "Kinship Network Analysis." *The SAGE Handbook of Social Network Analysis*, 533–49. https://doi.org/10.4135/9781446294413.n35.

Hamid, Mohsin. 2011. "Why Pakistan Will Survive." In *Pakistan: Beyond the Crisis State*, edited by Maleeha Lohdi, 35–44. London: Hurst & Company.

Hocart, Arthur Maurice. 1950. *Caste: A Comparative Study*. London: Methuen & Co. Ltf.

Holy, Ladislav. 1996. *Anthropological Perspectives on Kinship*. London: Pluto Press.

Humeira Iqtidar, and Noor Akbar. 2014. "Caught between Drones and Army Raids, Pakistanis in 'Tribal Areas' Feel Betrayed." *The Conversation*. 2014. https://theconversation.com/caught-between-drones-and-army-raids-pakistanis-in-tribal-areas-feel-betrayed-34216.

Jaffrelot, Christophe. 2006. "L'Inde, Démocratie Dynastique Ou Démocratie Lignagère?" *Critique Internationale* (33): 135–52. http://www.jstor.org/stable/24564647.

Jaffrelot, Christophe. 2015. *The Pakistan Paradox: Instability and Resilience.* Translated by Cynthia Schoch. London: Hurst and Co.

Jamieson, Mark. 1998. "Linguistic Innovation and Relationship Terminology in the Pearl Lagoon Basin of Nicaragua." *The Journal of the Royal Anthropological Institute* 4 (4): 713–30.

Javid, Hassan. 2011. "Class, Power, and Patronage: Landowners and Politics in Punjab." *History and Anthropology* 22 (3): 37–41. https://doi.org/10.1080/02757206.2011.595006.

Kaplan, Robert D. 2012. "What's Wrong with Pakistan? Answer." *Foreign Policy* (194): 94–99. http://www.jstor.org/stable/23242798.

Keiser, Lincoln. 1991. *Freinds by Day, Enemies by Night: Organized Vengeance in a Kohistani Community.* London: Holt, Rinehart and Winston Inc.

Khalifa, Rashad. 1989. *Quran: The Final Testament: (Authorized English Version): With the Arabic Text.* Tucson: Islamic Productions.

Khan, Iftikhas A., and Kalbe Ali. 2014. "The Mystery of Raiwind Palace Ownership." *Dawn*, January 3, 2014. www.dawn.com/news/1078082.

Khan, Reham. 2018. *Reham Khan.* SK Publishing.

Latour, Bruno. 1999. "Factures/Fractures: From the Concept of Network to the Concept of Attachment." *RES* 36: 20–31.

Leach, Edmund. 1962. *Aspects of Caste in South India, Ceylon and North-West Pakistan.* Cambridge: Cambridge University Press.

Leaf, Murray J. 1972. *Information and Behavior in a Sikh Village: Social Organization Reconsidered.* University of California Press.

Leaf, Murray J. 2007. "Empirical Formalism." *Structure and Dynamics.* http://escholarship.org/uc/item/851847x3.

Lemay-Hébert, Nicolas, and Stefanie Kappler. 2016. "What Attachment to Peace ? Exploring the Normative and Material Dimensions of Local Ownership in Peacebuilding." *Review of International Studies,* 42 (July 2011): 895–914. https://doi.org/10.1017/S0260210516000061.

Lévi-Strauss, Claude. 1963. *Structural Anthropology.* Basic Books.

Lieven, Anatol. 2011. *Pakistan: A Hard Country.* Allen Lane.

Lindholm, Charles. 1982. *Generosity and Jealousy: The Emotional Structure of a Competitive Society, Swat District, North Pakistan.* New York: Columbia University Press.

Llewellyn, Karl Nickerson, and Edward Adamson Hoebel. 1941. *The Cheyenne Way: Conflict and Case Law in Primitive Jurisprudence.* Norman: University of Oklahoma Press.

Lustick, Ian. 2011. "Secession of the Center: A Virtual Probe of the Prospects for Punjabi Secessionism in Pakistan and the Secession of Punjabistan." *Journal of Artificial Societies and Social Simulation* 14 (1): 7. https://doi.org/10.18564/jasss.1696.

Lyon, Stephen M. 2002. "Modelling Competing Contextual Rules: Conflict Resolution in Punjab, Pakistan." *Cybernetics and systems 2002: Proceedings of the Sixteenth European Meeting on Cybernetics and Systems Research.* Edited by R. Trappl, 1: 383–89. Vienna: Austrian Society for Cybernetics Studies.

Lyon, Stephen M. 2004a. "Modeling Context in Punjabi Conflict Resolution: Social Organizations as Context Agents." *Cybernetics and Systems* 35 (2–3). https://doi.org/10.1080/01969720490426867.

Lyon, Stephen M. 2004b. *An Anthropological Analysis of Local Politics and Patronage in a Pakistani Village*. Lampeter: Edwin Mellen Press.

Lyon, Stephen M. 2005. "Culture and Information: An Anthropological Examination of Communication in Cultura Domains in Pakistan." *Cybernetics and Systems: An International Journal* 36 (8): 919–32.

Lyon, Stephen M. 2013. "Networks and Kinship: Formal Models of Alliance, Descent, and Inheritance in a Pakistani Punjabi Village." *Social Science Computer Review* 31 (1): 45–55. https://doi.org/10.1177/0894439312453275.

Lyon, Stephen M. 2017. "On Brothers and Sisters: South Asian and Japanese Idea Systems and Their Consequences." *World Cultures* 22 (1). https://escholarship.org/uc/item/2f00s96z.

Lyon, Stephen M., and Muhammad Aurang Zeb Mughal. 2016. "Ties That Bind: Marital Networks and Politics in Punjab, Pakistan." *Structure and Dynamics: EJournal of Anthropological and Related Sciences* 9 (2): 110–22. http://escholarship.org/uc/item/5378v2fx.

Lyon, Stephen M., and Muhammad A. Z. Mughal. 2017. "Categories and Cultural Models of Nature in Northern Punjab, Pakistan." *World Cultures* 22 (2). https://escholarship.org/uc/item/77w806mp.

Lyon, Stephen M., and Muhammad Aurang Zeb Mughal. 2019. "Cultural Models of Nature and Divinity in a Rain Fed Farming Village of Punjab, Pakistan." In *Cultural Models of Nature Primary Food Producers and Climate Change*, edited by Giovanni Bennardo. 141–164. Oxford: Routledge.

Lyon, Stephen M., Mark A. Jamieson, and Michael D. Fischer. 2015. "Persistent Cultures: Miskitu Kinship Terminological Fluidity." *Structure and Dynamics: EJournal of Anthropological and Related Sciences* 8 (1). http://escholarship.org/uc/item/6w65n7sf.

MacMillan, Margaret. 2014. *The War That Ended in Peace*. Penguin Random House Trade Paperbacks.

Madsen, Stig Toft. 1991. "Clan, Kinship, and Panchayat Justice among the Jats of Western Uttar Pradesh." *Anthropos* 86 (4/6): 351–65. https://doi.org/10.2307/40463659.

Maine, Henry Sumner. 1861. *Ancient Law: Its Connection with the Early History of Society, and Its Relation to Modern Ideas*. London: J. Murray.

Malhotra, Inder. 2006. "Nehru's Luminous Legacy." *India International Centre Quarterly* 33 (3/4): 22–33. http://www.jstor.org/stable/23006066.

Manto, Saadat Hasan. 2001. *A Wet Afternoon: Stories, Sketches, Reminiscences*. Islamabad: Alhamra.

Marriott, McKim. 1976. "Hindu Transactions: Diversity without Dualism." In *Transaction and Meaning: Directions in the Anthropology of Exchange and Symbolic Behavior*, edited by Bruce Kapferer. 109–142. Philadelphia: Institute for the Study of Human Issues.

Marsden, Magnus. 2007. "All-Male Sonic Gatherings, Islamic Reform, and Masculinity in Northern Pakistan." *American Ethnologist* 34 (3): 473–90. http://www.jstor.org/stable/4496828.

Martin, Nicolas. 2014. "The Dark Side of Patronatge in the Pakistani Punjab." In *Patronage as Politics in South Asia*, edited by Anastasia Piliavsky, 326–45. Cambridge: Cambridge University Press.

Martin, Nicolas. 2016. *Politics, Landlords and Islam in Pakistan*. New York: Routledge.
Martin, Nicolas. 2018. "Corruption and Factionalism in Contemporary Punjab: An Ethnographic Account from Rural Malwa." *Modern Asian Studies* 52 (3): 942–70. https://doi.org/10.1017/S0026749X1700004X.
Mauss, Marcel. 1966. *The Gift*. London: Cohen & West Ltd.
McCartney, Matthew. 2019. "In a Desperate State: The Social Sciences and the Overdeveloped State in Pakistan 1950–1983." In *New Perspectives on Pakistan's Political Economy: State, Class and Social Change*, edited by Matthew McCartney and S. Akbar Zaidi, 25–55. Cambridge: Cambridge University Press.
Morgan, Lewis. 1870. *Systems of Consanguinity and Affinity of the Human Family. Smithsonian Contributions to Knowledge*. Vol. XVII. Smithsonian Institute.
Morgan, Lewis Henry. 1877. *Ancient Society; or, Researches in the Lines of Human Progress from Savagery, through Barbarism to Civilization*. New York: H. Holt.
Murdock, George Peter. 1971. "Anthropology's Mythology." *Proceedings of the Royal Anthropological Institute of Great Britain and Ireland* (1971): 17–24. https://doi.org/10.2307/3031759.
Niaz, Ilhan. 2010. *The Culture of Power and Governance of Pakistan 1947–2008*. Karachi: Oxford University Press.
Padgett, John F., and Christopher K. Ansell. 2008. "Robust Action and the Rise of the Medici, 1400–1434." *American Journal of Sociology* 98 (6): 1259–319. https://doi.org/10.1126/science.1165821.
Parkes, Peter. 2004. "Milk Kinship in Southeast Europe. Alternative Social Structures and Foster Relations in the Caucasus and the Balkans." *Social Anthropology* 12 (3): 341–58. https://doi.org/10.1017/S0964028204000540.
Parkes, Peter. 2005. "Milk Kinship in Islam. Substance, Structure, History." *Social Anthropology* 13 (3): 307–29. https://doi.org/10.1017/S0964028205001564.
Parkin, Robert. 1997. *Kinship: An Introduction to the Basic Concepts: An Introduction to Basic Concepts*. Oxford: Wiley-Blackwell.
Parkin, Robert, ed. 2004. *Kinship and Family: An Anthropological Reader (Wiley Blackwell Anthologies in Social and Cultural Anthropology)*. Malden; Oxford: Blackwell Publishing.
Pickett, Mark. 2013. *Caste and Kinship in a Modern Hindu Society: The Newar City of Lalitpur, Nepal*. Bangkok: Orchid Press Publishing.
Pretus, Clara, Nafees Hamid, Hammad Sheikh, Jeremy Ginges, Adolf Tobeña, Richard Davis, Oscar Vilarroya, and Scott Atran. 2018. "Neural and Behavioral Correlates of Sacred Values and Vulnerability to Violent Extremism." *Frontiers in Psychology* 9 (December). https://doi.org/10.3389/fpsyg.2018.02462.
Radcliffe-Brown, Alfred Reginald. 1957. *A Natural Science of Society*. New York: Free Press.
Read, Dwight. 2005. "Some Observations on Resilience and Robustness in Human Systems." *Cybernetics and Systems: An International Journal* 36 (8): 773–802.
Read, Dwight. 2013. "A New Approach to Forming a Typology of Kinship Terminology Systems: From Morgan and Murdock to the Present." *Structure and Dynamics: EJournal of Anthropological and Related Sciences* 6 (1). http://escholarship.org/uc/item/0ss6j8sh.

Read, Dwight W. 2001. "Formal Analysis of Kinship Terminologies and Its Relationship to What Constitutes Kinship." *Anthropological Theory* 1 (2): 239–67.
Read, Dwight W. 2006. "Kinship Algebra Expert System (KAES): A Software Implementation of a Cultural Theory." *Social Science Computer Review* 24 (1): 43–67.
Read, Dwight W., and Clifford A. Behrens. 1990. "KAES: An Expert System for the Algebraic Analysis of Kinship Terminologies." *Journal of Quantitative Anthropology* 2: 353–93.
Read, Dwight, Michael Fischer, and Murray Leaf. 2013. "What Are Kinship Terminologies, and Why Do We Care? A Computational Approach to Analyzing Symbolic Domains." *Social Science Computer Review* 31 (1): 16–44. https://doi.org/10.1177/0894439312455914.
Rivers, W. H. R. 1900. "A Genealogical Method of Collecting Social and Vital Statistics." *Journal of the Royal Anthropological Institute* 30: 74–82.
Robert, Parkin. 1998. "Dravidian and Iroqois in South Asia." In *Transformations of Kinship*, edited by Maurice Godelier, Thomas R. Trautmann, and Franklin E. Tjon Sie Fat, 252–70. Washington; London: Smithsonian Institution Press.
Sahlins, Marshall D. 1961. "The Segmentary Lineage: An Organization of Predatory Expansion." *American Anthropologist* 63 (2): 322–45. https://doi.org/10.1525/aa.1961.63.2.02a00050.
Schimmel, Annemarie. 1982. *Islam and India in Pakistan. Iconography of Religions, XXII*. Leiden: E. J. Brill.
Shaw, Alison. 2009. *Negotiating Risk: British Pakistani Experiences of Genetics*. Oxford; New York: Berghahn Books.
Shaw, Alison. 2011. "Risk and Reproductive Decisions: British Pakistani Couples' Responses to Genetic Counseling." *Social Science and Medicine* 73: 111–20. https://doi.org/10.1016/j.socscimed.2011.04.011.
Spear, Percival. 1967. "Nehru." *Modern Asian Studies* 1 (1): 15–29. http://www.jstor.org/stable/311582.
Sperber, Dan. 1985. "Anthropology and Psychology: Towards an Epidemiology of Representations." *Man* 20 (1): 73–89. http://www.jstor.org/stable/2802222.
Steward, Julian Haynes. 1955. *Theory of Culture Change: The Methodology of Multilinear Evolution*. Urbana: University of Illinois Press.
Stone, Linda, and Diane E. King. 2019. *Kinship and Gender: An Introduction*. 6th ed. New York: Routledge.
Talbot, Ian. 1996. *Khizr Tiwana, the Punjab Unionist Party and the Partition of India*. Surrey: Curzon. http://www.loc.gov/catdir/enhancements/fy0909/97101524-d.html.
Tharoor, Shashi. 2017. *Inglorious Empire: What the British Did to India*. London: C. Hurst & Co. (Publishers) Ltd.
Turner, Victor W. 1958. *Schism and Continuity in an African Society: A Study of Ndembu Village Life*. New York: The Humanities Press.
Verdon, Michel. 1981. "Kinship, Marriage, and the Family : An Operational Approach." *American Journal of Sociology* 86 (4): 796–818. http://www.jstor.org/stable/2778343.
Weller, Susan C., Ben Vickers, H. Russell Bernard, Alyssa M. Blackburn, Stephen Borgatti, Clarence C. Gravlee, and Jeffrey C. Johnson. 2018. "Open-Ended

Interview Questions and Saturation." Edited by Andrew Soundy. *PLoS ONE* 13 (6): e0198606. https://doi.org/10.1371/journal.pone.0198606.

Werbner, Pnina. 2003. *Pilgrims of Love: The Anthropology of a Global Sufi Cult.* Oxford: Oxford University Press.

Werbner, Pnina. 2010. "Notes from a Small Place: Anthropological Blues in the Face of Global Terror." *Current Anthropology* 51 (2): 193–221. http://www.jstor.org/stable/10.1086/651041.

Yaqoob, Malik. 2012. "Politics Runs in the Family – Newspaper – DAWN.COM." *Dawn*. 2012. https://www.dawn.com/news/773506.

Zahid, Shahid. 2013. "The Family Connection: How Social and Economic Development Is Linked to the Nature and Power of Political Dynasties." *The Herald*, no. Special Issue: Election 2013: 16–24.

Zaidi, Hassan Belal. 2016. "'Panama Papers' Reveal Sharif Family's 'Offshore Holdings.'" *Dawn*, April 4, 2016.

Zaidi, S. Akbar. 2014. "Rethinking Pakistan's Political Economy: Class, State, Power and Transition." *Economic and Political Weekly* 49 (5): 47–54.

Index

acephalous societies, 2–3, 12;
    Azande, 4;
    Cheyenne, 63, 127;
    Kazakh, 36;
    Netsilik Inuit, 14;
    Nuer, 3–4, 47, 125
affinal kin, 48, 58
Alexander the Great, 33
Ali ibn Abi Talib, 36, 53
alliance, 7, 29, 34, 36, 47, 50, 107, 114–15
aristocratic families, 11, 83, 120
attachment, 15–16

Bhutto family 92–95;
    Asif Ali Zardari, 52, 94, 101;
    Benazir Bhutto, 53, 94;
    Bilawal Bhutto Zardari, 52, 94–96 101;
    Murtaza Bhutto, 96;
    Shahnawaz Bhutto, 96;
    Zulfikar Ali Bhutto, 53, 69, 88, 92–94, 102
biradari, 19, 51, 52–53, 61, 70, 72, 75, 77–79, 100, 104, 116
blood feud, 63, 65

British Raj, 3–4, 6, 8–9, 12, 20, 33–34, 38–40, 41–43, 47, 49–50, 59, 72, 78, 80, 83, 92, 106, 109, 126, 130;
    Gazetteers, 65

caste, 5–6, 19, 33, 66–67, 115
conception, 37, 48, 51, 52, 54, 94
conflict mediation:
    jirga, 66–68, 71, 76;
    local conflicts, 63;
    panchayat, 66–67
corruption, 13, 9, 25, 101–2, 105–7, 122;
    David Cameron, 105;
    Panama Papers, 25, 105, 131
cousin marriage, 18, 52, 73–74
cousin rivalry, 65, 68

Daud, Baba Shaikh, 39–40
descent, 7, 18–19, 21, 29, 31, 35–38, 45, 47–50, 52–53, 55–56, 58, 61, 73, 84, 86–88, 104, 113–14, 115–16

ecosystems models, 14
empirical formalism, 113

factionalism, 9–10, 107
Federally Administered Tribal Areas, 65, 117

Gujerat Chaudhry family:
  Chaudhry Shujaat Hussain, 88–89, 96;
  Chaudhry Zahoor Elahi, 88, 110

Image of Limited Good, 75, 125
inheritance, 76–77
Ishaq Dar, 100
Israel, 7–8, 35, 108

Jinnah, Fatima, 84

Khan, Ayub, 45, 69, 84, 88, 97, 102, 112
Khan, Imran, 9, 11, 89, 95, 97, 101, 102, 104–9
Khan, Jemima (Goldsmith), 105, 107
kinship algebras, 17, 59
kinship terminologies, 2, 13, 17, 58, 59, 60

land registry, 30

Mahmud of Ghazni, 35
Maneka, Bushra, 108
masculinity, 57
maternal transmission, 48, 54, 57
Maussian gift, 65
Medici, 11, 120, 129
methods:
  animals in a row, 29;
  consent, 29;
  free listing, 29;
  genealogical data, 28;
  mapping genealogies, 57;
  participant-observation, 29;
  pedigrees, 30–31;
  pile sorting, 28;
  social network analysis, 29–31
Mianwali Niazi, 104

milk kinship, 36, 37;
  Qatar, 37
Miskitu, 13, 60, 128
Morgan, 16
MQM, 44, 101
Mughal Empire, 11, 4, 19, 33, 37–38, 41, 42, 44, 83, 124–25, 128

nasl, 37, 47, 52, 53, 57, 94
National Assembly of Pakistan, 85, 88, 101, 108
National Database & Registration Authority (NADRA), 30, 50
network analysis, 2, 4, 11, 15, 19–20, 22n1, 31, 33, 38, 45, 48, 74, 78, 82, 85, 86–90, 98, 100, 104, 116, 120
numberdar, 73, 80

the Pakistan Syndrome, 8
partition, 44
patrilineality, 48
personhood, 56–57, 60–61;
  Langkawi Malay, 17
political parties:
  ANP, 101;
  PML, 89, 90, 92, 100, 102, 105, 109, 116, 124;
  PML-N, 89–90, 100, 102, 105;
  PML-Q, 89–90, 102, 109;
  PPP, 89–90, 92, 94, 102, 116;
  PTI, 89, 101–2, 104–5, 107–9, 116
Provincially Administered Tribal Areas, 65
purdah, 37

Qadri, Mumtaz, 100

reciprocity, 11, 120–21
resilience, 13–14, 18, 21, 34, 36–37, 44–45, 64, 78, 109, 115, 121–22
robustness, 13, 14, 36, 78, 115

Sabra and Shatila massacres, 35
Sadiq, Major Tahir, 90, 91–92, 95, 109
shari'a courts, 67
Sharif, Shahbaz, 97, 100
Sharif family:
   Abbas Sharif, 98;
   Asma, 100;
   Begum Kulsoom, 98, 100;
   Captain Safdar, 98, 100, 111;
   Mian Muhammad Sharif, 98;
   Nawaz Sharif, 11, 25, 53, 90, 95–101, 105, 111;
   Shahbaz Sharif, 98;
   Thee Great Gama, 99, 111n1
sibling relationships, 40
Sikh Empire, 38, 39;
   Ranjit Singh, 38, 39, 40, 72

silsila, 53
structural functionalist anthropology, 3, 18
structuralism, 18
Suri, Sher Shah, 38, 104
Syria, 121–22

Taseer, Salman, 100
tax base, 11, 119–20
tribal politics, 36

Unionist Party, 80, 95, 109
Urdu kin terminology, 59

varna. *See* caste

Zia ul Haq, 45, 92, 97–98

About the Author

Stephen M. Lyon is an anthropologist who has carried out field research in rural and urban Pakistan since 1998. He is the professor of Anthropology at the Institute for the Study of Muslim Civilizations at the Aga Khan University (International) in London. Prior to taking up his position at AKU-ISMC, he was the chair of the Department of Anthropology at Durham University and the Deputy Director of the Durham Global Security Institute. He is the author of numerous publications on kinship, conflict, computational methods, and environmental anthropology in Pakistan. He has carried out applied anthropological research in collaboration with different development organizations based in Pakistan, the United Kingdom, and the United States.

Lightning Source UK Ltd.
Milton Keynes UK
UKHW041534021222
413268UK00016B/122